Library
Brevard Junior College
Cocoa, Florida

D1713804

An Anthology of Modern Hebrew Poetry

AN ANTHOLOGY OF MODERN HEBREW POETRY

edited by **ABRAHAM BIRMAN**

Foreword by MOSHÉ SHARETT

Library
Brevard Junior College
Cocoa. Florida

ABELARD-SCHUMAN

London   New York   Toronto

©*Copyright* 1968 by ABRAHAM BIRMAN

Library of Congress Catalogue Card Number: 68-16350
Standard Book No. 200.71419.8

LONDON
Abelard-Schuman
Limited
8 King St. WC2

NEW YORK
Abelard-Schuman
Limited
6 West 57 St.

TORONTO
Abelard-Schuman
Canada Limited
896 Queen St. W.

PRINTED IN THE UNITED STATES OF AMERICA

To my wife, Hadassah

31871

Acknowledgements

The editor wishes to acknowledge his indebtedness to the following translators: Bernard Lewis, Helena Frank, L. V. Snowman, Grace Goldin, Thomas Silk, L. Bernard, Hilda Auerbach, Leon Yudkin, Arthur Jacobs, Jacob Sloan, Dov Vardi, Ezra Spicehandler, Richard Flint, Nina De-Nur, Chayym Zeldis, Michael Bullock, Jon Silkin, David Saraph, Dom Moraes, Ruth Finer-Mintz, Meir Wieseltier, Maxim Ghilan, David Avidan, Miriam Arad, Dennis Silk, S. Solis-Cohen, I. Zangwill.

Grateful acknowledgement is made to the following authors, publishers and holders of copyright. Dr. L. V. Snowman for his translations from Bialik, taken from *Bialik, Poems from the Hebrew*, London, 1924; likewise for translations of Tchernikhovsky and Shneur, taken from the various sources. The Histadruth Ivrith of America for the translations from the *Complete Works of Bialik*, ed. Dr. Israel Efros, New York, 1948. To Chaim Rabbin and David Patterson for the excerpts from *Sifrut*, pub-

lished by the Jewish Agency, London. To Leon Yudkin for his
translations from Itzhak Lamdam, taken from Mr. Yudkin's M.A.
thesis. To Sifriat Poalim, Tel Aviv, for permission to translate
the poems by Yehudah Karni from *Songs of Jerusalem*. To J.
Sonntag, Editor of *The Jewish Quarterly*, London, for the ex-
cerpts from his journal. To Yehiel and Nina De-Nur for the
four excerpts from *The Clock Overhead*. To André Deutsch Ltd.,
Publishers, London, and to T. Carmi, Tel Aviv, for the poems
from *The Brass Serpent*, London, 1964. To Curtis Brown Ltd.,
London, for the excerpts from *The Wisdom of Israel*, ed. L.
Browne. To Ruth Finer-Mintz and Robert Zachary for the trans-
lations from Haim Gouri, taken from a forthcoming anthology
to be published by the University of California Press. To Dov
Vardi for permission to quote from his critical essays in his book
New Hebrew Poetry, Tel Aviv, 1947. To the Thirtieth Century
Publishing House; London — Tel Aviv, for the poems by David
Avidan. To the Institute for the Translation of Hebrew Literature
for several poems from their recent anthology published by the
Israel Universities Press. And to the following authors for their
kind permission to translate from their work and, in many cases,
for their active cooperation in revising the manuscript and send-
ing me translations to which I had no access in England: Abra-
ham Shlonsky, Shin Shalom, Leah Goldberg, Nathan Alterman,
Yehiel De-Nur, David Rokeah, T. Carmi, Haim Gouri, Yehudah
Amikhai, Nathan Zakh, Maxim Ghilan, David Avidan, Dan
Paggis, Dalia Ravikovitz, Moshé Dor, Ory Bernstein, Arnon Ben-
Nahum, Meir Wieseltier, Dalia Hertz.

Some of the poetry translations included in this volume were
published in the following periodicals in the English-speaking
countries and Israel: *Encounter, Commentary, Midstream, Jeru-
salem Post, Palestine Tribune, Antioch Review, Stand, Expres-
sion, Transatlantic Review, Modern Poetry in Translation, The
Times Literary Supplement, Israel Argosy, Sifrut, Israel, The
Jewish Quarterly*.

Contents

13

14

Foreword

By Moshé Sharett, M.K., formerly Prime Minister of Israel.

It is my pleasant duty to present to the English-speaking public *An Anthology of Modern Hebrew Poetry*, compiled and edited by Abraham Birman, an Israeli writer and translator who is now in England.

Owing to various reasons, especially difficulties of translation, Hebrew poetry is at present hardly accessible to the vast majority of cultured readers throughout the world. The influence of the Bible has always been a major factor, and our mediaeval literature was read and esteemed by many scholars in nearly all European countries. It is doubly deplorable, therefore, that this important link has been severed in recent times.

Today a large percentage of world Jewry resides in English-speaking countries and its connections with Israel must rely primarily on the English language. Furthermore, ever since it became an official language in Palestine, English has been close to many Israeli intellectuals. Our younger generation of poets, too, has been strongly influenced by English poetry and will be glad, I am sure, to offer something in return.

It is my sincere hope that the present anthology will help to acquaint readers in many countries with some of the treasures of our poetry and to rebuild the bridge between our culture and that of the wide world.

Jerusalem, 1965.

Note

In the period of time which has elapsed since the completion of this anthology, the death has occurred of Mr. Moshé Sharett.

I should like to express my heartfelt regret at this great loss to the Jewish people in general and to me in particular.

Abraham Birman

Preface

In presenting this anthology to the public, the editor would like to comment briefly on the difficulties entailed in the compilation of a collection of translated poems.

Anyone who has tried to translate poetry knows the fascination and the danger which confront him in this somewhat ungrateful task. In an anthology of translations, especially one that aims at a cross-section of a whole era, to have attempted to represent a foreign culture by slipshod renderings would be simply to malign it. Consequently, the exacting demands it was necessary to impose on the choice of translations precluded important poets like Uri Zvi Greenberg and Avot Yeshurun whose work is well-nigh untranslatable, and made the respective representation of included poets quite different from what it would be in a Hebrew anthology.

While every attempt was made to include many pieces of poetry germane to Jewish life and lore, and to facilitate their comprehension for the non-Jewish reader by means of a glossary and notes at the end of this volume, it was deemed better to forgo those poems which no amount of annotation could really explain. One can only hope that the Introduction, which begins at the Biblical era though the anthology itself starts with Bialik (1873-1934), will help the uninitiated to obtain an insight into the background of Jewish literary tradition in its many vicissitudes.

The editor wishes to single out for special thanks Mr. Moshé Sharett, M.K., His Excellency Arthur Lourie, the Ambassador of Israel in London, Professor Sir Isaiah Berlin, Professor Norman Bentwich, Sarah and Professor Aryeh Dvoretsky and Professor Chaim Rabin of the Hebrew University, Jerusalem, all of whom have helped with his fellowship to this country; and Doreen and Philip Rossdale, Dr. David Patterson, Arthur Jacobs, Maxim Ghilan and Meir Wieseltier for having read the manuscript and made very valuable suggestions. Likewise, his thanks are extended to all the authors, translators and publishers who have made this anthology possible.

London, 1967.   Abraham Birman

Introduction
THE DEVELOPMENT
OF HEBREW POETRY

I. The Evolution
of Jewish Consciousness
and Poetic Expression

Although this collection is entitled *An Anthology of Modern Hebrew Poetry,* it should be explained at the outset that the term 'modern,' as applied to the Hebrew language and verse, has a meaning quite different from that associated with English and other languages, old or new.

The main reasons for this difference are the unique history and mentality of the Jewish people and the way they affected its modes of expression. In order to follow this remarkable development we have to start at the very beginning.

The Old Testament, Israel's greatest literary heritage, already evinces a highly developed consciousness and sophistication. The Book of Genesis still contains some very ancient fragments, but from Exodus on we have a more or less clear picture of a nation past the tribal stage (though still divided into tribes), with traditions that go back to the days of Abraham, a nation set free from the bondage of Egypt and well on its way to the Promised Land.

It was at the beginning of the long desert trek that there occurred the first and most significant event in its annals: *Matan Toráh,** the Revelation of Mount Sinai. The Bible gives an im· pressive description of this epoch-making experience:

"Then the Eternal descended on the mountain of Sinai. . . . and the mountain of Sinai was all wrapped in smoke as the Eternal descended in fire upon it. The smoke rose like steam from a kiln till the people all trembled terribly."

(Exodus 19:18, Tr. James Moffatt)†

The Aggadah‡ strikes a more subtle but no less impressive note:

"When God gave the Torah not a bird twittered, not a wing stirred, not an ox bellowed, not a wheel flew, not a seraph said 'Holy,' the sea did not stir, people did not talk, the whole world was steeped in silence, till the Voice rang out: 'I am the Eternal, your God'."

(Shmot Rabba, 29)

By any account this event had an almost traumatic effect on the consciousness of the nation. Furthermore, the Torah laid numerous injunctions and inhibitions on the shoulders of its believers. It is true that, contrary to many primitive tribes, they were not supposed to live in constant dread of a fulminating deity: as long as they observed what was incumbent upon them they were promised a peaceful, rich and rewarding existence. But the five books of the Pentateuch are full of warnings as to what would happen if they strayed from the right path. These

* The accent on Hebrew words in this book merely denotes the stressed syllable.

†All quotations from the Old Testament in this Introduction are taken, by courtesy of Hodder & Stoughton Ltd., from James Moffatt's translation, unless otherwise specified.

‡See Part III of this Introduction.

warnings, culminating in the famous *Tokhekha** (Section of Reproof) abound with threats and curses:

. . . ."then shall all these curses come upon you and overtake you. Cursed shall you be in town and in country. Cursed your basket and kneading-trough . . . cursed shall you be when you start out and when you return home. . . .The Eternal will strike you with consumption, fever, ague and erysipelas, with drought, blasting and mildew, that shall pursue you until you perish; the sky overhead shall be brass and the earth underfoot shall be iron. . . .The Eternal will strike your minds with madness, blindness and dismay. . . .you shall be utterly crushed. . . .with no one to rescue you."

(*Deut.* 28)

The influence wielded by such a strong magnetic field was bound to turn all creative art into 'applied art.' Every new aspect of the nation's life was subjected to the acid test of the Torah's principles, and for every value that stood the test there were many that did not. The most vehement campaign was launched against those values that were associated with idolatry, and so adamant were our forefathers on this point that they forbade the sculpture of living images and looked askance at any aesthetic enjoyment of such art even when created by Gentiles. Love of Nature was not frowned upon as such, yet the Talmud† warns anyone who takes a walk in the countryside and admires the beauty of a tree that he has committed a mortal sin if this diverts his mind from study and contemplation. Likewise, strict priority was allotted to all things essential to the religious, spiritual and material needs of the community, and nearly everything else was dubbed trivial. Thus the laws and tenets of the Torah became a touchstone, a lodestone and a weighing-stone all rolled into one.

* The 'kh' in Hebrew words should be pronounced like the 'ch' in 'Bach.'

† See Glossary and General Notes at the end of this volume.

It was the combination of these two factors — the fusion of the old with the new and the insistence on unambiguous purposefulness — that made for 'applied art' in nearly all fields of creativity. It is true that this very lopsidedness brought about a unique sort of freedom, a somewhat slavish peace of mind fostered by the knowledge that obedience entails security, but the price was too high. Hebrew literature acquired a monolithic character and in the post-Biblical era some of it became too epigrammatic, too *pointée,* too wary of spontaneity. Worse still, spontaneous aspects were harnessed to a definite purpose, reminding one of Sir Walter Scott's "laborious mountains and scooped out glens and carefully ruined abbeys," as E. M. Forster so aptly puts it. Hebrew poetry became mainly 'occasional' and all too often marked occasion but did not make it.

The result of these influences was a powerful, edifying, memorable literature with few half-tones or half-shades, fewer doubts, misgivings or sceptical contemplations, and little or no bric-à-brac, light - verse or doggerel. Even the famous *Atz Kotzetz* which lent its very name to doggerel in Hebrew was not a farcical piece of verse but a description of intended persecutions. In many cases the Talmud frowned at jocularity except at the expense of idols and their worshippers. Light satire, the kind that 'deserves to be suppressed if understood by the censor,' was exceedingly rare. Savage satire, on the other hand, flourished from time immemorial and was mainly directed against the enemies of Israel. A fine example of taunting verse is that part in the *Song of Deborah* where she hurls ridicule at Sisera's mother who is waiting for her son, unaware that he has been defeated and slain:

> "Out of the window she leans and peers,
> Sisera's mother, out of the lattice:
> 'Why are his chariots lingering? Why?
> Why is the sound of his wheels so long?'
> And her ladies, so knowing, reply —
> 'They must be dividing the spoil they have taken,

A wench or two apiece,
Dyed robes for Sisera's share
And brocade and brocades for my neck.' "

(*Judges* 5:28-30)

All this does not mean that Hebrew literature was congealed, stuffy or cold-hearted: in the Bible, the Aggadah and elsewhere we find many warm passages with rare understanding of human nature. But wherever emotions came into conflict with the Law, written or unwritten, they were inevitably suppressed. *Yikkov HaDin Et HaHar*—literally 'let the Law pierce the mountain,' the Hebrew equivalent of *fiat justitia, ruat coelum*—stood unchallenged for well-nigh three thousand years. It is true that the Law itself was humane, respectful of human dignity and well ahead of those dark ages; but strict or lax, stern or considerate, it was built into the mechanism of the nation like a finely-adjusted gyroscope, rotating on one immutable axis.

The fusion of the old and new went on with astounding fluidity throughout the ages. Around Hebrew literature there hovered an aura of timelessness — not merely the prevalence of time-honoured concepts but a certainty that 'there is nothing new under the sun,' or stronger still, 'the more things change, the more they remain the same.' If for a creative artist like Bartok it was something of a discovery that 'we have to go to the very ' in order to achieve the very new,' it was commonplace to the jewish creative spirit. Indeed it had no need to *go* to the very old: the ancient concepts, beliefs, feelings and language made themselves felt at every corner. All values were constantly moulded and remoulded until they fitted perfectly, in form at least, into the general pattern.

In the centuries that followed, when the great majority of the nation was driven into exile, the hold of the Law became even more stringent. The Talmud with its numerous sequels had already been written down, and since the uniqueness of the Jewish people was now an important asset for sheer physical survival, all forms of creative art were diverted into vital but narrow channels, mainly the *Piyyut* and the *Aggadah*. Needs came before wishes, utility before inspiration. Jewish national escapism was directed *from* Nature into study and contemplation. There were to be no more prophets, and the prophetic spirit which somehow refused to die out assumed mystical forms like the Cabbalah, premature dreams of the Messiah, even licentious and orgiastic extremities so alien to the Jewish mind.

After a brilliant but short-lived renaissance in Spain, Italy and Provence, the Jewish people seem to have shrunk a bit in stature. This process was partly conscious, even intentional, as though a deep instinct whispered to the nation that it must turn itself into an ethnic, moral and social microcosm in order to survive the persecutions of the Dark Ages, which for them at least extended far into the nineteenth century. Daily life fell under the rule of mediocre and often narrow-minded men, although many minds of the first rank still made their appearance in the sphere of study. What remained of Jewish creative energy was primarily expressed in barren hairsplitting known as *pilpul* — casuistic ratiocination for its own sake. Even the study of the Bible as such was often discouraged and many people knew it mainly through Talmudic quotations. Those parts of the Bible that could not be ignored were given a scholastic or symbolic meaning, such as the *Song of Songs* which was now alleged to be an abstract love-relationship between God and Israel.

Yet life flowed on inside that microcosm which refused to fossilize or become a cocoon. In spite of appalling poverty, bitter persecution and the almost complete isolation of the Jews from the life of the populace, especially in Russia and Poland, the life of the Jewish community was dynamic and well-organized. The nation's vitality put up a passive but stubborn fight and the troubles of the individual were solaced by the affairs of the community, by study and charitable deeds. Suicide was rare, dissipation infrequent and innocuous, alcoholism virtually unknown in its extreme manifestations.

Nor did the creative spirit die out. In the Aggadah, in sermons and homilies, in jokes and *bon mots* (known all over the world and classified in some textbooks as a high form of art), in Yiddish folk tales and penny dreadfuls, creative fermentation found a constant outlet. At the end of the nineteenth century Yiddish literature rose to great heights and wielded an important influence on Hebrew prose and poetry.

All these centuries the Hebrew language was kept in a curious state of aggregation. On one hand it was never dead — at least the erudite élite was familiar with Hebrew and Aramaic. Since the Bible, the Mishnah and large tracts of the Aggadah were written in Hebrew, and since quotation was an integral part of their study as well as a favourite pastime, the scholars resorted almost daily to the ancient language. Moreover, the greater part of the prayers was in Hebrew, and though simple folk did not always understand the accurate meaning of the words, the number of those who did was relatively higher than the number of Catholics who knew the Latin of their prayers. Most important of all, the yearning for redemption was closely linked with the Hebrew language which was to revive and become universal with the advent of the Messiah. Paradoxically enough, this proved a stumbling block for the first attempts to resuscitate Hebrew as a spoken language, since such attempts were regarded as unholy endeavours to secularize the Holy Language and 'force the early coming of the Messiah.'

To sum up, the very forces which prevented Jewish life in exile from acquiring its full stature were the forces that saved it from extinction. By a marvellously well-adjusted balance between the old and new it was able to walk in many a valley of death and come out alive, and with the advent of the great revival it floated to the surface and once more sought its way to normal existence.

But before we describe the sequence of moods and events that led to the complete resuscitation of the Hebrew language and the renascence of its poetry, let us retrace our steps to the heritage of former ages and see how it developed in accordance with the principles enumerated above.

II. The Poetry
of the Old Testament

The Bible, which for our purpose will be taken to mean the Old Testament only, is formally divided in some English translations into prose and poetry. This division, formerly based on considerations of metre and prosody, would not always be compatible with modern requirements involving inner rhythm, emotional tension and the avoidance of rhetorical effects — criteria which might disqualify as poetry large tracts of the Book of Proverbs, parts of the Prophecies and even some of the Psalms on account of their ecclesiastic and didactic tendencies. On the other hand, many 'prose' passages such as the Section of Reproof quoted in Part I, or the Revelation of Mount Sinai, would now fall into the category of verse.

The beginnings of Biblical poetry are very ancient indeed, but even the first fragments are so vivid, so distinct in outline, that they remind the reader of Cro-Magnon artistry rather than ordinary primitive rites. The whole Book of Genesis is imbued with a sensitive if somewhat inarticulate culture that aims at edification as well as at description. Even the lengthy genealogical delineations have a grandeur of their own. The very first piece of personal poetry, *Lemekh's Song*, is sung in a comparatively restrained tone:

> "Adah and Zillah, listen to me.
> O wives of Lemekh, hear what I say:
> The man who wounds me, him I slay,
> I slay a boy for a blow."
>
> (*Gen.* 4:23)

Nearly all these 'occasional poems' are intensely personal. In *Jacob's Blessing*, for example, the dying father describes to his sons their different lots in the distant future, and the whole poem is permeated with enlightened clannishness. At the end of the Book of Deuteronomy we find a magnificent summing-up of the relationship between God and His Chosen People. The Desert Generation, however, receives a sound reproof for its sins:

> "Yeshurún fattened and grew restive,
> ay, you fattened, gross and gorged!
> They forsook God who had made them,
> scorned their steadfast One, their succour,
> stirred him to jealousy with their foreign gods,
> angered him with hateful idols."
>
> (*Deut.* 32:15-16)

When the people of Israel developed into an independent nation, culminating in the kingdom of David and Solomon, the amenities of 'normal' existence began to appeal very strongly to the great majority, conflicting more and more with the stern demands of the Law. This tendency was severely discouraged ('And it shall not come to pass. . . .that you would be like all other nations. . . . I shall rule you with an iron hand') and it was mainly the effort to suppress it that gave rise to the phenomenon known as prophecy.

Appraisal of the prophets and their work depends largely on one's point of view in religious matters, but it is evident even to the staunchest agnostic that they differed from ordinary people in one important sense: they could not and would not keep silent about things which the common man ignores, acquiesces in, even applauds. "A prophet who withholds his prophecy deserves to be killed," said the Aggadah, and often the things he could not withhold burst from his mouth with indignation and rose to a pitch that must have sounded shrill even to the Oriental ear:

> "Shriek away! 'Tis close, 'tis close, the Eternal's day.
>> as a mighty blow from the Almighty.
> Then shall all hands grow limp,
>> all hearts shall melt,
>>> and mortals be dismayed;
> Seized with pangs and throes they writhe
>> like a woman in her labour,
> staring at each other aghast,
>> their faces aflame."
>
> (*Isaiah* 14:6)

"Truth sung in a passion," as W. B. Yeats defined poetry, might have been the prophets' motto, and it was a very astringent brand of truth that they professed. It contradicted all conventional concepts of convenience, the majority rule or the whim of rulers. They did not shrink from reproaching a king for his sins, as Nathan reproached David for what he had done to Uriah the Hittite, and it is worthy of notice that taking the "poor man's ewe lamb" was deemed an even worse offence than David's adultery with Bathsheba.

One of the many striking features about the prophets is their almost complete self-effacement. The little that Jeremiah, for example, has to say about himself makes us doubt whether he at least had any personal world of his own. Not only was he shunned by his playmates in childhood and by his fellow-men in adulthood, but even when he was alone his thoughts revolved eternally round his duties to the Lord:

"I never joined the jesting band,
    I never rioted.
I sat alone under thy hand,
    sharing all thine indignation."

(Jer. 15:17)

The prophecies of Jeremiah, the most human and lovable of
them all, are mostly set in a minor key. His reproach is blended
with paternal affection and deep expressiveness. The sins of
Israel do not seem to him so much abhorrent as pointless, almost
unnatural:

"Can a girl forget her trinkets
    or a bride her sash?
And yet my people have forgotten me
    days without number."

(Jer. 2:32)

With unfailing accuracy he predicted the destruction that was
to result from nothing more formidable than a petty political
intrigue, and lived to see the First Temple destroyed. Far from
rubbing it in, however, he began to preach redemption and con-
solation and joined the exiles to comfort them in their hour of
grief.

Alone of all the great prophets, he complains about his bitter
lot, but at his worst moments he could not relinquish his duty,
try as he would:

"If I say, I will not mention it, I will not
    speak in his name any more,
then I feel within me as it were a fire
    that burns my very being.
I am tired of this,
    so tired I cannot bear it any longer."

(Jer. 20:9)

Like Job he goes so far as to curse the day he was born and the very circumstances of his birth:

> "Cursed be the man who told my father
> crying, 'A son is born to you!'
> and giving him joy.
> May that man fare as fared the towns
> that the Eternal pitilessly crushed.
> May he hear shrieks at dawn
> and the battle-cry at noon
> because he did not stifle me in the womb."
>
> (Jer. 20:15-17)

If Jeremiah presents a picture of a sensitive, great-hearted man dedicated from birth to his task, we see in Job (Eyob)* a carefree and prosperous person crushed overnight by tragedy. As he sits amid dust and ashes, scratching and bewailing his ulcers like Henley's poor old tramp, his three friends come to visit him from far-off lands and, after a decent interval of silence, reproach him for his faithlessness. Eliphaz the Temanite, the most poetically-minded of the whole group, describes his own revelation that made him trust in the judgement of the Lord:

> "Once a word came stealing to me,
>   the whisper of it reached my ear.
> When men fall into trances in the night,
>   rapt, I lay in my visions.
> Terror and trembling seized me
>   till my limbs all shuddered;
> a spirit glided before me
>   till my hair was bristling —
> there it stood!"
>
> (Job 4:12-16)

---

* Job (Eyob) is regarded as a prophet in the Aggadah (and by the Moslems) but not in the Bible. Rabbi S. D. Sassoon — a relative of the poet, Siegfried Sassoon — has recently offered the interesting theory that it was Jeremiah who wrote the Book of Job as well as the Psalms and the Book of Proverbs.

The great drama of Job, which treats life as an enigma, comes closer to our concept of 'pure' poetry, though it is still bounded by moral and theological considerations. Its exquisite blend of realism and mysticism is strongly manifested when the Lord answers Job out of the storm in a passage singularly free from melodramatic effects:

"Can you pull out Leviathan with a hook
or tie his tongue down with a cord?
Can you pierce his nose with a reed
or his cheek with a thorn?
Will he throw a supplication to you?
Will he speak soft words to you?
Will he make a treaty with you
to become your eternal slave?
Will you play with him as with a pet bird
or cage him for your maidens?"

(*Job* 41:1-5, adapted version)

The Book of Ecclesiastes is brimming with the worldly, *blasé* over-sophisticated (though not quite cynical) disenchantment of a sage who has seen and tasted too much of life. The whole book echoes the subtle melancholy of the opening words: "Vanity of Vanities, says the Preacher." Even when the author offers advice it is with a weary shrug of self-mockery, yet his scepticism is not entirely nihilistic or rebellious. He soberly advises young men to enjoy life in their salad days but remember that retribution lies in store for them. He might have subscribed to such wishful thinking as *"si jeunesse savait, si vieillesse pouvait."*

He had a quiet horror of old age and death, and in a solemn passage described the disintegration that comes with senility:

"When the keepers of the house shall tremble,
and the strong men shall bow themselves, and
the grinders cease because they are few, and
those that look out of the windows be darkened.

32

"And the doors shall be shut in the streets. . . .
and all the daughters of musick shall be brought low.

". . . and the grasshopper shall be a burden,*
and desire shall fail; because man goeth to
his long home, and the mourners go about the streets.

"Or ever the silver cord be loosed, or the golden
bowl be broken, or the pitcher be broken at the
fountain, or the wheel broken at the cistern."

(*Eccl.* 12:3-6, authorized version)

The Book of Ecclesiastes, probably the last book of the Old Testament in chronological order, marks the transition from a period of boldly sculptured, monolithic poetry to a quieter, more subdued era whose strong emotions had to flow in undercurrent, sometimes underground channels. The chief artistic creation of this new epoch was the *Aggadáh*.

* This metaphor is supposed to portray the deterioration of sexual powers.

III. The Poetry of the Aggadah

The term *Aggadáh*, which means a legend or a folk tale, has been expanded and generalized in Jewish consciousness to mean almost everything that is not canonical law, known as *Halakháh*. Under the category of Aggadah come the legends, fables, tales, proverbs, reflections, piquant or intriguing stories, moral and ethical observations, mysticism and demonology. All these are included in the Talmud and in smaller collections, particularly the *Midrashim* (singular *Midrash*), which were almost exclusively dedicated to the Aggadah.

The Halakhah and Aggadah were not contradictory but complementary concepts which overlapped in a good many cases. The two, says Bialik, differ only in their state of aggregation, like ice and water. An even more apt definition was given along these lines by Shmariahu Levin: "If the Halakhah is an ocean, the Aggadah is the Gulf Stream that flows through it." To this warm source of consolation and encouragement the heart of the nation turned in distress, and the more frequent and bitter the persecutions became, the more it strengthened its bond with the Aggadah.

This unique literary form has been compared by our sages to roses, to apples, to spices and perfumes, yet they saw in it not only a thing of great beauty and a balm to the ailing soul but an important auxiliary to study and contemplation. They treated it as a combination of hyacinths and biscuits, to paraphrase Carl Sandburg's definition of poetry, and we may note in passing that Sandburg is an eminent folklorist in his own right. The Jewish masses were not slow to catch up with the élite in their admiration of this mode of expression, transmitted to them through sermons and homilies, and though the scholars were reluctant to teach it to 'the ignorant and simple-minded,' their efforts to limit its popular appeal were not crowned with success.

A considerable part of the Aggadah was based on the scriptures of the Bible. The favourite technique, known as *Drash*, was to build a story, legend or fable round a scripture, usually by playing upon its words and attaching to them a meaning or connotation different from the ordinary one, known as *Pshat*. All too often the *Drash* was far-fetched even for a fanciful mind, but at its best the Aggadah managed to capture the spirit, if not the letter, of the original scripture and throw a new light on it. Those post-Freudians who maintain that dreams and even actions are based not only on the regular motivations of the subconscious but also on chance words heard or overheard during waking hours, will find the word-play of the Aggadah an interesting study.

For all its moderation and forbearance the Aggadah never shrank from debunking the nation's heroes when they deserved it. Just as the Bible made no bones about the sins of leaders like Saul and David, so the Aggadah often enlarged upon their weaknesses or the preposterous situations in which they found themselves from time to time:

> " 'And Saul swore [to the witch] by the Lord, saying as the Lord liveth there shall be no punishment in this for you.' [*Sam. I.* 28:10]. Said Resh Lakish: 'This may be likened to

a woman who spends the night with her lover yet swears by the life of her husband. Did not Saul go to a witch and swear by the Lord!' "

(Vayyikra Rabba, 26)

Even the prose of the Aggadah is lifted, by virtue of its conciseness and perspicuity, into a class by itself, offering the refined but earthy taste of semolina as against the daily bread of the Halakhah. But there are large tracts whose originality and aesthetic perception place them high in the ranks of 'pure' poetry:

> "If you would like to know how great was the beauty of Rabbi Yohannan, take a silver bowl, fill it with pomegranate grains, encase it in a wreath of roses and place it on the borderline between sun and shadow. And that splendour is but a faint image of Rabbi Yohannan's beauty."

(B.M., 84)

Quite often the Aggadah was well ahead of its time in intuitive observation. Nearly two thousand years before Darwin one sage made a striking remark, "The birds were created out of the mire, and the proof of this is that they have scales on their legs like fish." In style and thought one can find innovations that smack of twentieth century cubism: "Nothing is more rectangular than the six days of Creation." Ethically, too, our sages ventured to propose laws that seem Utopian even now: "You can be forced to do your neighbour a good turn if you don't stand to lose anything."

Even to God the Aggadah ascribed human traits and weaknesses, though always with the proviso that they be taken metaphorically. It dryly remarks, for example, that when God wanted to redeem the people of Israel He told Moses, "Go bring *my* people out of Egypt," but when they worshipped the Calf of Gold the Lord said, "Get away. . . .for *your* people have depraved themselves." There is also the famous story about Moses in his final hour, utterly devoid of stoicism and even common dignity, bargaining with God and entreating Him desperately to postpone the inevitable.

It is on the subject of death that the Aggadah has some of its finest poetry to offer. Here the 'still small voice' makes itself heard 'from one end of the world to the other, like the passing of a soul.' There is the story of that grand old man, the blind Rav Sheshet, who was strolling one day in the marketplace when he met the Angel of Death and knew that his hour had come. "What! Here in the market?" he said. "Like a beast of burden? Come to my house." Formally this episode does not fall into the category of poetry, yet its intensity and fortitude remind us of Browning's defiant words at the beginning of *Prospice*:

"Fear death? — to feel the fog in my throat,
    The mist in my face,
When the snows begin, and the blasts denote
    I am nearing the place,
The power of the night, the press of the storm,
    The post of the foe;
Where he stands, the Arch Fear in a visible form,
    Yet the strong man must go."

True to its sense of dignity the Aggadah frowned on excessive mourning. "He who mourns too much over his dead is really bewailing his own death," it says, giving short shrift to self-pity. It has no taste for the macabre except where ethical values are at stake:

"After death the mouth and the belly start quarrelling.
Says the mouth to the belly, 'Every theft and robbery
that I have committed was only meant to keep you full.'
In three days' time the belly bursts open and says to
the mouth, 'Here is everything you have given me.' "

This highly ethical but somewhat unsavoury process is described from an amoral angle by a modern Israeli poet, David Avidan, to illustrate his favourite subject, disintegration:

"And the kidneys that secretly toiled
To restore what the brain had spoiled
Heard everything else recede
Saw everything else secede."

(from *Post Mortem, Tr.* A.B.)

It is this preoccupation with ethical values that lifts the prose
and poetry of the Aggadah far above the folklore, demonology
and mythology of those times. With telescopic clarity it reflects
the virtuous and austere outlook that was part and parcel of
Jewish life throughout the Diaspora. It seldom conforms to the
ordinary rules of poetry, much less to its conventions and
mannerisms, yet poetry it is — lucid and concentrated and very
much alive.

In recent times the best of this important literary heritage
was compiled by H. N. Bialik and Y. H. Ravnitsky into an
anthology of rare architectural beauty called *Sefer Ha'Aggadah*
— The Book of the Aggadah — which has already become a
classic of its kind, a much-used reference book and a compulsory
textbook in Israel from elementary school onwards.

In modern Israel the Aggadah played a prominent part in the
revival of the Hebrew language. Its peculiar zest and succinct-
ness added substantially to the 'pep' and trenchant wit for
which the Jewish people are world-famous. On the other hand,
its strict conciseness, basic matter-of-factness and lack of
turgidity helped to free Hebrew poetry from its time-old en-
slavement to rhetoric — a process which is by no means over —
and establish the 'non-solemn verse' that prefers sense to sound,
integrity to eloquence.

IV. Hebrew Religious and Secular Poetry in the Middle Ages

Alongside the Aggadah, and superseding it as an outlet for poetic creativity, Hebrew religious poetry flourished for almost a thousand years. Strictly speaking, it was divided into several categories such as the *Piyyut* (liturgical poetry), *Selihāh* (penitential poetry), *Kināh* (elegiac poetry) and so forth. But gradually the term *Piyyut* — which comes from the same Greek root as 'poetry' — came to mean any sort of poem which serves a religious purpose.

The most striking feature of the Piyyut at its best is its complete self-effacement, a quality in which it excels even more than the work of the prophets. Not only are its mood, tone, rhyme and acrostic intricacies subjected to non-secular purposes, where self-assertion would be a grave offence, but the very soul of the *Paytán* (writer of the Piyyut) seems to bend in effusive yet dignified supplication. A Piyyut is poetry wrapped in a prayer shawl:

"My soul into a cavern of despair is thrust
When I see all cities flourish in sin and lust
While the City of God is grovelling in the dust —
Yet to Him we belong and in Him we trust."
          (Amitai Ben-Shefatiáh, ninth century A.D., *Tr.* A.B.)

This kind of self-effacement implies no self-degradation, no acquiescence in individual or national tragedy. Often the Piyyut had bitter things to say about the plight of Israel and sometimes its remonstrances reached a high pitch, yet it was nearly always the anguish of a tortured soul, not the self-assertion of a bruised ego:

"Six years were decreed for a slave to wait
When his freedom he sought at his master's hand.
But the years of *my* bondage lack term or date —
It is hard, O my Master, to understand."
          (S. Ibn-Gabirol, *Tr.* Israel Zangwill)

Even those Piyyutim that do not rank among the best have a cumulative intensity which cannot be proved or disproved by quotation. Indeed the reader should be well-versed in this genre to appreciate the delicate fabric underlying the ornate embroidery of rhymes, acrostics, alliterations and other poetic paraphernalia. These very accessories produce a pathetic effect of their own, as if they too were meant to glorify the Lord by 'fireworks and fizgigs,' like the juggling tricks which that poor wretch performed before the altar of the Virgin Mary in a well-known story by Anatole France.

Some Paytanim invested so much craftsmanship in their work, that their 'applied art' acquired a selfless freedom of its own. So flawlessly did they depict the Creator that — as the Aggadah rather fondly points out — it was as though they had actually created Him. The more they humbled themselves before the Lord, the more it appeared that Man was a remarkable creature indeed if he could practise self-effacement with such rare skill:

"Like a piece of clay in the potter's hand,
At will to shorten, at will to expand,
So are we in your grip, God, Thou noble and grand.
    Look to the Covenant, not to desire.

Like the helm that a sailor can wield with ease,
At will hold tight and at will release,
So are we in your hand, God of kindness and peace.
    Look to the Covenant, not to desire."

                     (*Tr.* A.B.)

If the Aggadah was the Gulf Stream in the ocean of Jewish life and thought, the Piyyutim were the deep waves that kept surging upwards from the depths of its disturbed existence. While the Aggadah sustained the nation's soul, the Piyyut served as an outlet for its hope of redemption and helped build a defensive inner pressure against the outer one which could be formidable. A poetry so inebriated with the glory of God — though often prolix and effusive — could hardly degenerate into that shoddy sentimentality so prevalent among poets who resort to similar techniques for a less elevated purpose.

Apart from the Piyyutim and other *Shiréi Kodesh* (Poems of Holiness), Hebrew mediaeval poetry is roughly divisible into two main categories: *Shiréi Tsión* (Songs of Zion) and *Shiréi Khol* (non-religious poetry). The first category comprises poems which were not incorporated into religious ritual yet expressed the woes of Zion and the fervent hope for redemption. The second category includes poems of nature, contemplation, war and peace, amatory verse — all that would come today under the heading of secular poetry. Because of the great adversity in which the Jewish people lived most of the time it was only for very brief periods that secular poetry attained a foothold, let alone an equal footing, with religious and redemptory verse.

The all too brief renaissance in Spain, Italy and Provence, where the Jews enjoyed for a time a climate of comparative tolerance and where individuals rose to prominence among the

Moslems and Christians, saw a galaxy of Hebrew poets, scholars, and philosophers, the most important of whom were Shlomó (Solomon) Ibn-Gabirol, Yehudah Ha'Levi, Moshé Ibn-Ezra, Abraham Ibn-Ezra and Emmanuel of Rome.

Little is known about the short life (c.1010-c.1050) of Shlomó Ibn-Gabirol. He was born in Malaga, Spain, and brought up in Saragossa. Orphaned at an early age, he was forced to rely upon the favours of patrons and other benefactors and this, together with a severe affliction of the skin, made him a touchy, irascible person. He had a genius for making enemies and alienating friends and indulged freely in polemics, calling his rivals and critics "the thorns and briars of the earth." His opinion of himself was far from modest:

"If the world does not make me leader and chief
It is loth to perform a loving feat.
Had it known my true merit it would have lief
Prostrated itself before my feet."

This 'style of the big I' absorbed much of Ibn-Gabirol's energies and spoiled large tracts of his personal poetry. When it comes to religious poetry, however, his self-effacement is all the more remarkable for the huge areas of self he has to efface, and the praise which he lavishes upon the Almighty exceeds by far any praise he may have lavished upon himself. True to Jewish tradition, he puts his whole personality behind his intercession for weak, sinful man:

"O Lord, what is man?
Wooden, harassed, frail.
Like straw he shall crack
Under thrashers' flails.
If ever you tax
Him with sin's full bale

He shall melt like wax
And crawl like a snail.
So, merciful God,
Be not strict but lax."

(*Tr.* A.B.)

As his talent matured, Ibn-Gabirol's spontaneous glorification of God was supplanted by a more recondite form, culminating in his famous *Keter Malkhut* (The Kingly Crown), a long poem of forty chapters with a sprawling but very delicate, perspicuous and coherent architecture. Again it is that inebriated preoccupation with all things celestial that elevates this poem to a level far higher than that of a philosophic treatise in verse. It is interesting to compare the following passage with the stanza of *Lord, what is man* quoted above and to note the difference in tone, colour and maturity of thought:

"From the day of his birth man is hard-pressed and
    harrowed,
Stricken, smitten of God and afflicted.
His youth is chaff driven by the wind,
His old age is flying straw,
And his life withers like a herb,
And God joins in hunting him.
From the day he comes forth from his mother's womb
His night is sorrow and his day is sighing.
If today he is exalted
Tomorrow he shall crawl with worms.
A grain of chaff puts him to flight
And a thorn wounds him.
If he is sated he waxes wicked,
And if he is hungry he sins for a loaf of bread.
His steps are swift to pursue riches
But he forgets Death who is after him."

(*Tr.* Israel Zangwill)

The life and work of Yehudah Ha'Levi (c.1075 – c.1145) could have been much more tranquil than that of Ibn-Gabirol, had it not been for the consuming love of Zion which became an obsession towards the end of his life. He was born in Spain where he studied and practised medicine and wrote poems, commentaries and philosophic treatises. Although his professional and literary reputation must have been prominent, his soul knew no rest as long as he was far away from the Holy Land. Pious as he was, the hope of redemption in the far-off future was not enough for him. In his deeply moving *Ode to Zion* — which Goethe is said to have ranked as one of the most impressive poems in world literature — his genuine pathos reaches its climax:

> "Your air is balm to the soul, your dust sweet as myrrh,
> Your rivers resound like harps and viols.
> Naked and barefoot would I walk amid temples
> Fallen into ruin and stopped with briars,
> Where the Holy Ark was hidden and where
> Your angels dwelt and your priests sang in choirs.
> Let me trample my worldly riches and curse the fate
> That profaned in alien lands your godly scions.
> How can I relish my food and drink
> When I see that the hounds are mangling your lions?
> Or how can daylight be sweet to my eyes
> When the ravens are feeding on the eagles of Zion?"
>
> (*excerpts, Tr.* A.B.)

Unlike some of his friends who preferred to worship Zion from a safe distance, Yehudah Ha'Levi was as good as his word. When he was over sixty years old he set out for the Holy Land. It is known that he reached Egypt safely but from that point on everything is surmise. In all probability he reached his destination and either died or was killed there.

Although this voyage — a hazardous undertaking in those days — filled the poet's soul with rare enthusiasm (reaching its summit on the way from Egypt to Palestine where 'wild wolves appealed to him as virgins appeal to boys') the preliminary stages must have taken some soul-searching. In his famous poem which begins with the words 'Shall you chase youth when you are fifty' he exhorts himself to relinquish his worldly affairs and set out on the long-contemplated pilgrimage:

"And do not take fright in the midst of the sea
When you see whole mountains in deadly throes,
When the hands of the sailors shall melt like salt
And the craftsmen shall cringe like does,
And they who have blithely ventured forth
Shall reel from the tempest's blows.
The ocean pulls like a dragnet
And none can escape its woes.
The rigging is crushed like rubble
And the boards are bent like bows.
The storm's hand plays with the waters
Like corn-sheaves on threshing-floors:
One moment it piles them in stacks
The other it hoards them in stores.
And the same waves that rear like lions
Crawl snake-like when sapped of their force."

(*Tr.* A.B.)

The love-songs, or rather amatory verse, that Yehudah Ha'Levi wrote in abundance seem to have suffered more than his Songs of Zion from the bondage of Arabic forms and conventions. The style is too facile, the solutions too easy, the associations a trifle too obvious. Even the following passage, short and delicate as it is, has emotionally committed the sin of saying too much:

"Wake, my darling, from thy slumbers,
Wake and fill the room with bliss.
Did you dream some daring lover
Ravished from thy lips a kiss?

I am skilled in dreams and omens,
And thy vision, dear, means — this!"
(*Tr*. S. Solis-Cohen)

His epigrammatic light verse fared much better. Here Arabic influence is often a positive asset, and the combination of Arab subtlety and Jewish wit produces delightful yet profound verses which, for all their ostensible frivolity, have a serious kernel:

I

"He saw his likeness, agog,
As I dandled him on my knee
And kissed my eyes — the rogue! —
His image he kissed, not me."

II

"I spied a white hair in my beard
And plucked it out. 'Well done,' it sneered.
'You nipped a scout in one fell swoop,
But will you hold against my troop?'"
(*Tr*. A.B.)

These forms were further developed by Emmanuel of Rome (Immanuel di Roma, c.1270-1330), an acquaintance of Dante, who introduced the sonnet into Hebrew and wrote many religious poems, some of which are still used in synagogue ritual. But apart from these solemn preoccupations he utilized his talents and poetic innovations for more frivolous purposes, producing verses that sound quite innocuous to our generation but must have been anathema to the pious Jews of his age:

"How often does my inmost soul induce me
To waive my share in Paradise, since Hell
Alone can offer what I love so well:
Sweet nectar, damsels waiting to seduce me.

Whom shall I find in Paradise to love me?
A ghastly harridan? A beasty hag?
A sinless, pitch-black spinster dressed in rags,
Her righteous boredom towering above me?

Why should I seek you, Heaven, when you shelter
A host of nincompoops and crippled creatures?
I deem your pleasures nothingness and naught.

And Hell I hail, whose inmates do not swelter
In good deeds, where gazelles have lovely features,
And all its nooks with love and joy are fraught."

(*Tr.* A.B.)

It is fairly obvious that Emmanuel's bark was far worse than
his bite, and we may safely wager that he did not indulge in
one tenth of the carnal pleasures he was so fond of depicting.
His efforts were primarily aimed at satire, where in addition to
the traditional methods of the Roman classics he was one of the
first European writers to realize, six hundred years before Ed-
ward Lear and Lewis Carroll, the immense power of 'nonsense
literature.' In one of his poems he tells us how, when summoned
as doctor to a spoiled highborn lady, he saw her cover her pulse
with a piece of cloth, apparently expecting him to feel it through
the wrapping! Whereupon he hastened to put a heavy brick on
the cloth, felt the pulse through a frying pan and urged the
lady's relatives to "take some wolves' horns, marble juice, lunar
lustre, chickens' milk, a pit's shadow, the smell of frankincense, a
frog's tail, simmer all these ingredients in a waxen vessel, throw
in a mule's twins for good measure, spread the ensuing paste
upon an ant's skin and make of it a bandage for her ladyship's
belly."

This prescription sounds mordant indeed until we remember
that in those days a doctor was often required to kiss the hand
of his highborn patient, male or female, before he could proceed
with the treatment. Perhaps Emmanuel's bizarre methods of

ridicule were the result of his good nature, for he lacked the ingrained bitterness of a savage satirist. He chose to poke fun at human foibles in a rather refined way, without denouncing them. In his poem about Lord Ephron, that worthy satrap who drank only wine and never a drop of water, and who swore that if the Flood were made of wine and not water he would wish to be a Jonah's fish a-swimming in it, this kind of light-headedness strikes a genuine note:

> " 'O friends, make haste, no moment waste, and if you love my soul
> Go fetch me wine of Hélbon in my lordly silver bowl.
> O that's the thing to heart a king and make a sick man whole,
> But soil it not and spoil it not with water.'
> . . . .
> Lord Ephron, peace upon his soul, lies rotting in the dust
> Until that day when, sages say, the sinful and the just
> Shall rise to meet their due reward. Then let us meekly trust
> Nor he nor we shall crave in Hell for water."
>
> (*Tr.* S. Solis-Cohen)

The poetry of Moshé (Moses) Ibn-Ezra, though not of the same order as that of Ibn-Gabirol or Yehudah Ha'Levi, excels in tender thoughts and lyrical imagery. His poems, especially those that deal with Nature, rely less on rhetorical effects and more on first-hand impressions:

> "I went out into the garden in the morning dusk
> When sorrow was heavy upon me like a cloud;
> And the breeze brought to my nostrils the odour of spices
> As balm of healing for a sick soul —
> Then a sudden dawn flamed in the sky like lightning
> And its thunder surged like the cry of a woman that gives birth."
>
> (*Tr.* S. Solis-Cohen)

Like most of his contemporaries Moshé Ibn-Ezra wrote epigrammatic verses but on the whole preferred succinct meditation to pyrotechnic effects. Some of these verses are so quiet and contemplative that, as Arthur Clutton-Brock said about W. H. Hudson, writing for him seems a means of expressing what he would never say aloud:

"Remember, my friend, that death
Is a decree none can rescind.
While you think you are at rest
Your sap is slowly thinned.
You're like a man who lies quiet
Aboard a ship wafted by the wind."
(*Tr.* A.B.)

His kinsman, Abraham Ibn-Ezra, about whom Robert Browning wrote his famous poem *Rabbi Ben-Ezra,* presents the most versatile figure in Jewish mediaeval history. Poet, grammarian, philosopher, exegete, astronomer and mathematician, he knew every art and craft under the sun except how to provide for himself. He wandered from place to place, pursued by a maddening combination of spreading fame and persistent ill-luck, about which he complains like a true forerunner of Heine:

"An evil fate pursues me
    With unrelenting spite.
If I sold lamps and candles
    The sun would shine all night.

I cannot, cannot prosper,
    No matter what I try.
Were selling shrouds my business,
    No man would ever die!"
(*Tr.* S. Solis-Cohen)

It would perhaps be fitting to choose the last excerpt of this era from a much less known author, Yedaiah Ha'Penini, the greatest part of whose work followed conventional trends, but who occasionally managed to produce passages with a surprisingly modern ring. In his poem *The Speaking Soul*, written in free verse, the soul of man speaks with informal dignity akin to that of Whitman:

> "I lie among you like the fleece on the thirsty ground.*
> When there is plenty of dew the fleece will be soaked
> While the ground remains dry. Then, when she shakes off
>   her spray,
> The ground will benefit a little from her close proximity.
> But when the fleece, for all its lassitude and sponginess, is
>   dry,
> How can there be dew on the weary ground?
> So it is with me: while my path is straight and bountiful
> I shall thrive in His shadow and you shall profit from my
>   bliss.
> But when you ignore me and don an ephemeral mask,
> When you grovel in Ophir's mud and soil yourselves with
>   golden ore,
> When you become turncoats and join my inveterate
>   enemies —
> How easily will my thread of grace snap,
> How easily shall I fall prey to overwhelming odds!"
>
> (*Tr.* A.B.)

Hebrew mediaeval literature was well-known and esteemed in the Christian world — sometimes in its original language, sometimes through a series of translations that were often anything but accurate — and its echoes can be traced in the work of many modern writers. Cervantes, Milton, Browning, Heine, Edmond Fleg, Isaac Babel, Kafka and many others, all were

* See *Judges* 6:36-40.

familiar with some of the treasures of the Aggadah and, in a few cases, with Hebrew mediaeval poetry and philosophy. Just as Jewish picturesque types and ways of life excited the creative imagination of Rembrandt and Max Liebermann, so the peculiar savour of Jewish literature did not pass unnoticed by Christian writers and those Jewish writers who wrote in the mother-tongues of their respective countries.

The constant fusion of the old with the new, described in the preceding parts of this Introduction, was continued throughout the Middle Ages. Biblical and Talmudic ideas, moods and linguistic expressions, some of them already thousands of years old, were constantly brought to the surface by means of quotations, allusions or mystical references. Incidentally, this is the main reason why Hebrew mediaeval poetry suffers in translation much more than the poetry of any other period. All that the anthologist can hope for is to give the reader a bird's-eye view of the rare spirit, the enthusiasm, *esprit,* emotion and subtle wit that went into the making of the Piyyut, the secular poetry and the Songs of Zion.

V. The Emancipation
and the Haskalah Poetry

The nadir of Jewish intellectual and literary life, described at the end of Part I, stretched approximately from the end of the thirteenth century to the middle of the nineteenth. It was never a state of complete ignorance and obscurantism, but as far as poetry was concerned it could be written off as an almost total loss. From the beginning of the eighteenth century on there were glimmers of secular poetry in Italy, Germany, Poland and Russia, but these attempts — though they did keep the flame alive — were tepid and lackadaisical. Their main ingredients, as Bialik commented rather ruefully, were 'a little honey, a little balsam and a lot of sweat.'

With the advent of the Emancipation, proclaimed by Napoleon and continued in the West, though not always smoothly, two trends of life and thought made their appearance in European Jewry. In Western Europe the great majority were 'assimilationists' who regarded themselves as ordinary citizens with a religion different from that of their compatriots, and for whom Hebrew served only as an ancillary language for ritual purposes. In rare cases some of them wrote poetry in Hebrew but most of them preferred their native tongues.

In Eastern Europe, where civil rights were still denied to the Jews, the forces of emancipation from ghetto life concentrated on cultural enlightment known as *Haskalah*. For the Jews of Russia and Poland this was no abstract feast of reason but fresh water, if not oxygen, to their culture-starved minds. Once the floodgates were thrown open there was no holding them back. Books on secular subjects were gobbled up by intellects that Talmudic casuistry had sharpened to a razor's edge, languages were studied as if they were life-saving codes, dictionaries memorized from A to Z like choice morsels of poetry. Many *littérateurs* and even laymen began to write verses in Hebrew and here and there bold attempts were made to speak it in addition to Yiddish or to the local tongue. These early experiments proved a great help to the famous Eliezer Ben-Yehudah who was the first to speak Hebrew exclusively and bring up his children on no other tongue.

The literature of the Haskalah, devoted to a cause of enlightment which seems a bit naive nowadays but was vital for its time, served its purpose in the best possible manner but only a small portion of its poetry is still readable. Many writers used rather hackneyed Biblical language in their lyrical and pastoral poems, but when they wrote about everyday life they did not hesitate to draw on the language of the Aggadah and Halakhah and resort to Aramaic expressions. We shall mention in brief only two writers of this important transition period.

Mikhah Yosef Lebenson (1828-1852), known as 'Mikhál,' who died of consumption at twenty-four, wrote tender lyrical poems and a few Biblical ballads, the best of which is *Samson's Revenge*. The betrayed hero has fallen into the hands of the Philistines and has been blinded and put to work as a helpless slave, yet they are still afraid of him:

> "Thus when a captured lion is brought into the cage
> Tired, mangled, lying helpless in the net,
> But still his head moves, still his eyes blaze in rage —
> His captor is terrified yet."

A more formidable figure was Yehudah Leib Gordon (1830-1892), known by his initials as *Yalag*. When he turned from his pastoral ruminations to the problems of his day, especially when he attacked the petty pundits, the narrow-minded politicians and the intellectual parasites that abounded in Jewish life, his satire was as savage and unrelenting as that of Pope and Swift at their best. His poem *Kotzo Shel Yod* ('All Because of a Jot') is a long and biassed but artistic tirade against the bitter lot of the Jewish woman in general and the good and beautiful Bat-Shúa in particular. Her husband, Hillel, was an erudite lay-about:

> "He has eyes like a calf, he has ringlets like tails,
> A haggard face with a nondescript stubble —
> But his trenchant wit can thrash like a flail
> And grind whole mountains into rubble."

Unable to support his family Hillel went overseas and later agreed, for a consideration, to divorce his wife who had fallen in love with a better man. The local Rabbi, however, decreed the bill of divorce void for no better reason than a missing jot! Nor could a new certificate be obtained from Hillel, who had been drowned in the meanwhile with no proof of his death, and according to the Jewish law Bat-Shúa could never marry again.

Though Yalag's extreme views about the supposed callousness of the Rabbi were largely erroneous, the poem evinces an amount of empathy that gives it a vitality akin to real life, although it does not pass the supreme test formulated by Archibald MacLeish, "A poem should not mean but be."

With Yalag and his followers, Hebrew poetry began to throb again on the threshold of existence. They imbued it with zest and ardour, applied to it the criteria of European verse and prepared the way for a galaxy of poets whose art was of high quality by any standard. In prose this victory was achieved earlier with the work of Mendeleh Mokher Sefarim (Shalom

Yaakov Abramovitz, 1836-1918), but in poetry it remained for Mendeleh's disciple, Hayyim Nahman Bialik, to accomplish the task. "It takes a thousand prophesiers to produce one prophet," says Bialik in one of his essays, and it seems a touch of poetic justice that the man who coined such a fine maxim should be the first real poet to emerge out of the ranks of those 'literary labourers' who seldom made the grade but whose tireless efforts turned Hebrew literature again into a going concern.

VI. The Triumvirate: Bialik, Tchernikhovsky, Shneur

Hayyim Nahman Bialik was born in 1873 in the small village of Radi, province of Vohlynia, Russia. When his father died the boy was taken to his grandfather's home in the city of Zhitomir, where he received an orthodox education, but being a precocious child he also managed to steep himself in the works of contemporary Jewish writers, particularly those of the *Haskalah*. Later he went to the famous *Yeshivah* (Rabbinical Seminary) at Volozhin, and while still a student there he began to write poetry.

In 1893 he moved to Odessa where an important centre of Hebrew culture had just been set up. After a few years of great adversity, from which he was rescued by friends in the nick of time, he established himself as editor, publisher and an eminent authority on Hebrew literature. After the Revolution he moved to Berlin and from there to Tel Aviv, where he resided until his death in 1934.

The poverty of his early life is reflected in many of his poems, overshadowing much of the splendour of his childhood which was spent in beautiful surroundings. He sings about 'the

cricket, poet of squalor,' about the sordid hopelessness of Jewish
life. Even when he comes back after many years, hoping to find
some change, he finds none:

"Here again is the wizened hag,
    Knitting socks and fumbling,
Her mouth with oaths and curses filled,
    Her lips for ever mumbling.

Our cat is there: he has not stirred
    From his quarters in the house,
But in his oven dream he makes
    A treaty with a mouse."

(*On My Return*, Tr. L. V. Snowman)

While he recognizes that adversity may make a strong-willed
individual really great, he knows that this is only partly true of
a nation, that there is a limit beyond which it cannot 'buy air
for breath, steal light for the eyes.' At times he wonders
whether the term 'nation' or even 'a living organism' still applies.
Have not the great hopes raised by the Age of Enlightenment
proved false, at least for the victims of the pogroms? Have not
the Jewish people become like wilted grass? Can the dead stir
when the ram's horn sounds?

These morbid thoughts gained strength after Bialik's visit to
Kishinev, where a most cruel pogrom had just taken place. In
his long poem *The City of Slaughter* he describes the terrible
aftermath of this pogrom, and the poor remnants of the
slaughter appear to him a thousand times more dead than those
who have perished under the killers' hands:

"No lustre in the eye, no hoping in the mind,
They grope to seek support they shall not find:
Thus when the oil is gone the wick still sends its smoke,
Thus does an old beast of burden still bear its yoke.
Would that misfortune had left them some small solace
Sustaining the soul, consoling their grey hairs!"

(*Tr.* A. M. Klein)

The effect of these horrors on the nation's soul troubled Bialik far more than that of the physical and social sufferings, and it is against this kind of deterioration that his *Songs of Wrath* — of which *The City of Slaughter* is one of the most important— were unleashed with a fury almost unparalleled in Jewish and world literature:

> "Surely this too is a judgement of God and a great
>   reckoning,
> That you deny your own hearts;
> You cast your holy tears into every puddle
> And string them on every beam of false light,
> Pour out your mind over outlandish marble
> And sink your spirit into the bosom of an alien stone.
> And while your flesh drips blood between the teeth of your
>   devourers
> You stuff your soul too down their throats."
>
> *(Tr.* Jessie Sampter*)*

Much has been written about Bialik's 'prophetic' qualities, and one of the most outstanding similarities between his work and theirs is that like so many of them, notably Jeremiah, he was forced by circumstances to express much more vehement feelings than those which his mind and temperament would have prescribed under normal conditions. Had he been born into an ordinary nation he would have been content to write quiet, introspective poetry, though he would have undoubtedly raised his voice in defence of the underdog as Shelley did for the *Bees of England* and Thomas Hood for the poor seamstress in *The Song of the Shirt.* In Bialik's *Songs of Wrath,* magnificent as most of them are, the 'still small voice' is often stifled or, worse still, asserts itself in the midst of blood-dripping passages like a cricket in the morgue. Aware of the discrepancy between his social and artistic conscience, the poet is frankly envious of those who live quietly and express their thoughts humbly or not at all:

"Meek of the earth, humble in wit and works,
Unknown and unseen dreamers, mute of soul,
Stinted in speech, of beauty most abundant,
Privily embroidering your lives —
God grant my part and portion be with you.

Like coral of the reaches of the sea
The pleasant savour of your minds lies hidden
And blooms your nobleness like berries wild
Burgeoning in the shadow of a wood."

(*Tr.* A. M. Klein)

Unlike the prophets of old, Bialik was not primarily concerned with morals or religion but with the fossilization, the lack of sensitivity, the almost complete loss of self-respect that prevailed during the interim period when the forces of the *Haskalah* had shattered the old bastions — the Synagogue and the House of Study — and before the new forces of national consciousness could be brought to bear on at least a part of the Jewish people. His pathos, his relentlessness, his superb vision, all these 'prophetic' qualities were mainly utilized to galvanize whatever forces still lay dormant in the ethnic and linguistic sphere. Apart from his great erudition Bialik had a gift of discovering a hidden source of life where it was least suspected. Important as his own linguistic innovations are (they include words from totally different fields of life such as the Hebrew for aircraft, firefly, reaction, earth-connection, etc.) they are but a small part of the large stock of half-forgotten expressions that he brought to the fore and adapted to the new needs.

Bialik's style is structurally Biblical, but the minutiae of his craft, the lush expressions, the juicy idioms, the benevolent wisdom of an ancient race, all borrow largely from the *Aggadah* that his own anthology has helped to popularize throughout the Jewish world. Like all great authors he was incapable of slavish imitation and all foreign influences on his work, notably that of the eminent Russian poet Nekrassov, were transmuted into an unmistakably Hebraic medium. He excelled in that kind of emulation in which people quote others only the better to express themselves.

Bialik also wrote essays, legends and short stories and translated Cervantes' *Don Quixote* and Schiller's *Wilhelm Tell*. In an attempt to anticipate the full revival of Hebrew — which would come, as he often emphasized, only with the resuscitation of the spoken language — he created his famous folk-songs at a time when nobody thought or felt in Hebrew to the extent of producing such homespun fabric. If the height of all art is the creation of something out of nothing, these songs may be regarded as the pinnacle of Bialik's genius. Many of them were set to music and are still sung in Israel and elsewhere. Even the switch from Ashkenazic to Sephardic Hebrew, which changed the place of the accent in a good many words and all but nullified the lifework of most minor poets, failed to dislodge Bialik's poems and folk-gems from the place they had won in the nation's heart. He had become a classic in his own lifetime.

Saul Tchernikhovsky (1875-1943) was born in Russia. Unlike most Jewish writers his mother-tongue was Russian, not Yiddish, and his Hebrew studies were begun at a comparatively late age. He received a classical education, acquired a sound knowledge of several languages and studied medicine at Heidelberg. During World War I he served with the Russian army as a medical officer. After the war he lived in a number of countries, including Germany, and finally settled in Palestine where he received the honorary citizenship of Tel Aviv. He never relinquished his profession as a doctor, and his medical knowledge and insight were reflected in his poetry as well as in other literary activities. These included the compilation of a Hebrew-English-Latin medical dictionary at a time when Hebrew scientific terminology had to be half invented, half unearthed from almost forgotten sources.

A large part of his creative energy was dedicated to translations from ancient and contemporary poetry into Hebrew. His main achievements were the translations of the Assyrian epic *Gilgamesh,* the *Iliad* and *Odyssey,* extracts from Shakespeare's plays, Longfellow's *Hiawatha* and poems by Horace, Goethe, Shelley, Heine, Pushkin, De Musset and Francis Thompson. He was one of the first Hebrew writers to be influenced directly by English literature. His own poetry was widely translated into English and other languages.

He had a strong masculine personality but not a domineering one. His poetry was influenced by the classics he knew so well but was equally imbued with Jewish spirit, though the latter was ingrained in him not in the traditional manner but through some strange atavism, as it were, a kind of short-cut that enabled him 'to carry the Song of Songs in his heart.' He disliked casuistry for its own sake, yet his lengthy but charming *Idylls* have a bitter-sweet argumentative quality that also characterized him as a conversationalist.

Tchernikhovsky was much preoccupied with 'pagan' themes and his poetical pantheism was widely discussed, praised, condemned or ignored by various critics. Undeniably, poems like *In Front of Apollo's Statue* deal with such themes and have that passion for beauty that is associated with ancient Greece and that restraining discipline ascribed to Rome, but the *spirit* remains unmistakably Jewish, as Bialik astutely observes in his essay 'Our Young Poetry' which deals with Tchernikhovsky and other poets of his generation:

> "Do they sometimes pronounce the names of other gods? Let us not take fright. This is perhaps the last shred of rhetoric to which they still pay lip-service. Their real deity is the God of Israel and no other."

About pogroms and other manifestations of the nation's tragedies Tchernikhovsky could express himself quite forcibly, but his anger lacks the lofty pathos of Bialik's poems or the savage ruthlessness of Shneur and Jacob Kahan. It is usually a quiet, dignified anger, all the more effective for its discipline:

"There are many like him there—unsymbolled heap
'Gainst which the ox will trip that treads the wheat,
And the farmer curse in anger as he ploughs;
His skull in a mound, or grasshoppers' retreat

Before the autumn. Only clouds will weep
Cold tears for him, the storm still him with scorn,
No prayers be said for him but these laments.
Footpaths will pass him by, but none to mourn."
                    (from *Memorial to the Victims of the Ukraine,*
                                        Tr. L. V. Snowman)

There is one important exception to Tchernikhovsky's dis-
cipline and restraint. In his long poem *Barukh of Magentza*
(Mayence) he describes the ordeal and revenge of a Jew who
is forced by the Crusaders to become a Christian and kills his
two daughters to save them from a similar fate. But the invective
which Barukh hurls at the murderers, as well as the description
of the revenge that he perpetrates upon them by setting fire to
the church, are less impressive than those passages in which he
talks to his slaughtered wife with the perfect quietude of a man
whose tragedy has unseated his reason:

"And why, my darling, did you flee
Into the darkness of the pit?
Arise and we shall go and see
How merrily the town is lit.
It's cold here, but beside the hearth
Our daughters, full of joy and mirth
Await us both with tinkling bells.
But we must hurry, dear, or else
Their hearts will break with care and woe.
Arise, my darling, let us go!"
                                        (*Tr.* A.B.)

In his more serene poetry Tchernikhovsky developed an
idyllic-lyrical style that seldom resorts to the easier felicities of

rhyme and rhythm yet moves well, rather like a heavy bicycle that rolls smoothly on a good road. His descriptions of the Russian landscape tend to show that despite his sincere Zionism he still yearned for the picturesque amenities of this wide, fertile country. Even when he depicted the landscape of Palestine his pen was still guided by such sights as forests, broad rivers and a fertility of land that are still wishful thinking in the Israel of our day. This course has been followed by many young Israeli writers, some of whom have never seen Europe, who go on using these symbols of the Diaspora landscape which have a very real meaning for them.

Yet Tchernikhovsky could be subtle and scientifically accurate in his description of natural phenomena. He wrote a long poem about the bees, *The Golden People,* which vindicates the old maxim that a good piece of poetry will stand the closest analysis. Even where his intentions are primarily human, as in *Behold O Earth,* we are impressed by the plenitude of his mind:

"Behold, O Earth, how wasteful we have been.
Within your sacred lap, the secret dwelling-place, we hid
    our seeds. No more
The glossy barley-spray, the heavy-kernelled wheat,
The gold-streaked grain of rye, the tasselled sheaf of corn.

"Behold, O Earth, how wasteful we have been.
We have hidden the fairest of our flowers in you.
Those whom only the earliest rays of the sun have seen,
Whether retiring bud, or spray full of petalled incense,
Scarcely they knew of noon-tide, for their grief was
    innocence,
And before the dewdrops were dried they were caught in a
    light that was new."

(*Tr.* Hilda Auerbach)

Zalman Shneur (Russia, 1887 — New York, 1959), rightly called 'poet of passion,' spent most of his youth in the Slavic countries, but his travels during his unusually long *Wanderjahre* took him to many other places including Israel and the United States. He wrote an incredible amount of poetry and prose, much of which was translated into English and other languages.

He was a strikingly handsome man, even in his seventies, thus vindicating Oscar Wilde's remark that the tragedy of old age is not in being old but in being young. He possessed physical and mental strength to a remarkable degree. Everything about him was bigger than life-size, yet he had enough trenchancy and intellectual honesty to avoid rudeness and grossness. He is a true follower of 'the style of the big I,' but unlike Ibn-Gabirol he has no religious tenets before which his ego can stop short. His descriptions are sanguine and lurid, like Gaugin's pictures in the last years of his life, and like the celebrated French painter he was a frank voluptuary. But even about most sensual moments his manner of writing was not that of a playboy or a lecher, but rather that of a primitive chieftain whose assertive masculinity forbids him to show respect for the other sex:

"A little demon hid his tiny sting
Among the shrines of love, remorse and lust.
I whispered *I'm your slave* but was a king
And she — a wench that grovelled in the dust."

(*Prayer*)

When he does yield to his finer instincts he can be surprisingly tender, as in his poem *Husband and Wife*. There is genuine love between the middle-aged husband and his young wife, but her love is gay and carefree and his is silent and grave. When she tries to cheer him up he says that he would put her to the test — lead her to the top of a mountain and drop her in a sledge to the cheering crowd below:

"And I shall wait on the summit and see
Whether you'll stay at the valley's edge
Or climb the steep slope, carrying on your shoulder
This light and brilliant sledge.

Then, only then shall I believe, my darling,
That your husband is not just a big toy to you
Or a sad-hearted puppet. Then shall I kneel down
And on my bald head you can put your shoe."

He has a wholesome contempt for righteousness. It is much
easier, says he, to be a petty and righteous man than a great
and wicked one. He has no respect for passive martyrs — an
attitude diametrically opposed to that of traditional Judaism —
and sometimes goes out of his way to present them in a gro-
tesque, macabre light:

"At midnight the village idiot crouched on the lifeless jelly
That had been the Rabbi and now lay there, with its own
    blood smeared,
And tickled his upturned heel and pulled at his mud-
    stained beard,
And with sudden vehemence leapt up and kicked his back
    and belly:

'Get up, you souse, up to prayer! In the dirty ditch
You've fallen asleep, half-dressed, bare-headed, in vomit
    and grime.
O dear, what a sight. Where are your shoes, your *shtreiml*?*
Look at you, rolling here in the dirt like a drunken bitch!' "
                                                    (*Tr.* A.B.)

Though he lacked Tchernikhovsky's secular erudition and
analytic powers, Shneur had intuitive prowess bordering on the
uncanny. Among other things he predicted the finding of the
Dead Sea Scrolls. More famous is his prognosis — at a time when
pogroms were confined to certain parts of Russia and when the
West enjoyed a heyday of liberalism — that the Middle Ages
were soon to return. And like H. G. Wells who predicted the

* *Shtreiml* — A broad felt hat worn by orthodox Jews in Eastern
Europe at that time.

atomic bomb, Shneur lived to see his terrible prophecy come true. His poems about the holocaust and its aftermath, however, fall short of his preliminary warning, *The Dark Ages Draw Near*:

> "Again the Dark Ages draw near. Do you hear, do you feel, man of spirit,
> The stir of the whirling dust, the distant odour of brimstone?
> And oppressive foreboding hid in the air, in the heart, in the land,
> As at times of eclipse of the sun when houses grow pale, seem to quake,
> And the blue of the skies turns to lead, and the cattle start lowing with fear,
> And herbs and trees become pallid like foliage grown in cellars,
> And the faces of men are rigid, grotesque as masks of wax?"
>
> (*Tr.* L. V. Snowman)

It is not easy to sum up Shneur's role in the resuscitation of Hebrew poetry. Unlike Bialik and Tchernikhovsky he was not a master-builder, except perhaps in his Hassidic themes where he made a noteworthy contribution to the literary field of this important domain, as I. L. Peretz did in his short stories and Martin Buber in his contemplative prose. Even in his novels he seldom manages to curb his wild instincts, and all too often we have the impression that his left hand will soon demolish what his right hand has just tried to build. Yet his poetry served as a powerful catalyst in the process of revival and his style was like a strong, cleansing wind that shook the pillars of Hebrew culture.

Apart from his powers of prediction there was another aspect to Shneur's 'prophetic' quality. In his book *Aspects of the Novel*, E. M. Forster offers an original definition of this aspect for the prose writer, and with a few modifications we can use it for our own purpose:

"His theme is the universe, or something universal, but he is not necessarily going to 'say' anything about the universe; he proposes to sing, and the strangeness of his song arising in the halls of fiction is bound to give us a shock. How will song combine with the furniture of common sense? we shall ask ourselves, and shall have to answer 'not too well': the singer does not always have room for his gestures, the table and chairs get broken, and the novel through which bardic influence has passed often has a wrecked air, like a drawing-room after an earthquake or a children's party."

VII. The Poetry of
Avraham Shlonsky
Leah Goldberg, and
Shin Shalom

Avraham Shlonsky (1900-   ) was born in the province of
Poltava, Russia. He spent a part of his boyhood in Tel Aviv and
was thus the first poet to acquire a secondary education in
Hebrew. Returning to Palestine after World War I he lived
for a few years in a *kibbutz* and later did manual work in Tel
Aviv. After a year in Paris he joined the staff of the daily *Davar*
in Tel Aviv as a writer and journalist, and later became editor
of various modernist and progressive periodicals which broke
with the traditional trends yet managed to preserve the Hebraic
spirit of old. At present he is one of the chief editors of *Sifriat
Poalim* (Workers' Library), an important publishing house be-
longing to the left wing of the Israeli Labour Movement. He
translated many works of world literature, notably Shakespeare's
Hamlet and Pushkin's *Eugene Onegin*, and in collaboration with
Leah Goldberg compiled an excellent anthology of Russian verse
in Hebrew, much of which was his own translation.

With the advent of Shlonsky's poetry, Hebrew literature
entered its 'modernistic' phase. When he arrived on the scene at
the beginning of the 1920's, Hebrew had already become one of

the three official languages in mandatory Palestine, along with English and Arabic, and was cheerfully spoken by the majority of the younger generation who paid no attention to the numerous difficulties it still had to overcome. The writings of the 'triumvirate' — Bialik, Tchernikhovsky and Shneur — as well as those of Shimoni, Jacob Kahan, Jacob Steinberg and others, became standard texts and were held in awe by most poets and critics, who refused to deviate from the teachings of the masters. In all fairness to the older poets it must be said that they often did their best to encourage the young lions to stand on their own feet, and it was mainly these embryo rebels who soon outgrew their rebelliousness and reverted to the good old-fashioned style. It was against this self-imposed slavishness, abetted by most editors and critics, that Shlonsky launched his revolt, though in retrospect it seems as if he had overaccomplished his purpose. The style, mannerisms and modes of expression that he created and advocated in his new periodicals became a cult, almost a fetish among the young *littérateurs,* and a modernistic cult can be much stricter than a traditional one.

The Hebrew language, at any rate, benefited without reservation from Shlonsky's work. New terms, idioms, stock phrases, words invented or unearthed, in all these things he was at least as creative as Bialik. Whereas Bialik, especially in his poetry, aimed at a slow, deliberate, edifying growth of the language, Shlonsky handled it like a linguistic Edison, turning out inventions by the bushel and making the newly-resuscitated tongue perform difficult acrobatics — some of which would have been quite a feat even for the English language — before it could run or even walk well. Alterman said about him that he had always been both a lodestone and a pelting-stone to Hebrew. Yet the old-new tongue took everything smilingly in her stride.

Now that most of these innovations have become part of the language, we are sometimes conscious of a discrepancy between Shlonsky the linguist and translator and Shlonsky the poet. He might have benefited from Chesterton's postulate that poetry cannot express anything that is not ingrained in our pattern of associations, that it can be original only as far as it concerns itself with origins. It is perhaps an ironical twist of fate that the best of Shlonsky's poems are not those crammed with new-fangled stuff (which 'dates' the fastest) but those that, while stamped with his hallmark, are written in a more traditional manner:

"The room here is right-angled, as in all hotels,
But very long
And not too high
And narrow.
Here in the gloom you manage all too well
To whisper 'God' in adolescent terror.

To press a torrid brow against a window-pane
(The eye, you know, can hear at such an hour),
And like a dog whose master has been slain
Frustrated silence in the darkness howls."

(from *A Hotel Room, Tr.* A.B.)

Like nearly all poets, Shlonsky constantly revisits his child-hood. It must have been happier than Bialik's, for his nostalgia is of a lighter kind. One of his poems on this theme opens with a merry piccolo tune:

"We had tiny feet
(Mummy-daddy's joy, God's little chicklets).
O how we loved to dip them in the puddles
And watch them wallow in the mud like piglets."

(*Tr.* A.B.)

Shlonsky yielded to the needs of linguistic development at least as many temperamental concessions as Bialik did to the demands of national survival, and if this took a rather heavy toll of his Muse it made him a staunch Hebraist. His inner world of intellect and emotion was influenced, especially in his early stages, by Russian and French poetry, but his symbolism and imagery are largely borrowed from the Bible and the Aggadah or invented in the same spirit. Though strongly affected by the October Revolution, he never became a *bezbozhnik* (a spitefully godless person). Perhaps no Jew can ever become one, no matter how much of an agnostic he is. Shlonsky challenges the order of creation so boldly and eloquently, so much like Rabbi Levi-Itzhak of Berditchev who used to intercede before God for the people of Israel like an aggressive lawyer in court, that we seem to behold the Eternal smile in the best tradition of the Aggadah and say, "You have beaten me, my son."

In his poem *The End of the Nights* Shlonsky criticizes the overdiligence of the Creator and begs Him to be a little less of a perfectionist in His attitude toward frail humans:

"Everything goes into hiding yet dazzles.
Everything screams 'I exist not' yet stays.
Everything falters, too baffled to frazzle
Your X-raying gaze.

Is that why we quailed, sorely tempted to run
Away from the good and succumb to the wicked?
If only we managed, O Tangible One,
To take our eyes off the trigger!

But you, too, are weary of playing acquitter
And once more ensnare us, hellbound.
And once more a steely-eyed boa-constrictor
Is holding us riveted, spellbound."

Strong language indeed, ostensibly overstepping the limit of reasonable intercession, but on closer scrutiny we find an undercurrent of faith and reconciliation, though not unconditional surrender:

"Stop gazing at us like a hostile surgeon,
Besprinkle in us every fibre and root.
O teach us to smile on our birth like a burgeon,
At death to be still like the garnered fruit."

(*Tr.* A.B.)

A considerable part of Shlonsky's work deals directly or indirectly with physical toil, building, pioneering and unemployment. Most of it is 'applied poetry' in a new and refreshing sense. In several poems he eulogizes his own body in no ambiguous terms, but must be absolved of the charge of narcissism on the grounds that physical toil, especially in a *kibbutz*, was something of a cult in those days, as sacred and self-effacing as the old religious rites. When the poet says "Dress me, mother dear, in a coat of splendid colours, and lead me to work with dawn," he is not rhapsodizing or showing off but consecrating himself to perform a divine duty. At times the symbols of work reach the dimensions of abstract art:

"Here's the hint of murder,
Here's the blade pressing forward,
Here's Cain who the unity of clod dares defy.
Never was distance so gaugeable, finite,
Between man
And camel
And sky."

(*Tiller of the Ground, Tr.* Dov Vardi)

It is only in the last decade or so, when the majority of Israeli poets are firmly ensconced behind their urban café tables, that they are willing to admit that the 'saga of toil' has produced little more than a handful of really good poetry. There are the warm, endearing poems of Rahél, of whom it has been said that she is not a big star but a very near one. There are the prolix, highly idealized but very lovable '*Idylls*' of David Shimoni (Shimonovitz), a trifle oversweet to the palate, though it is always the sweetness of honey without a grain of saccharine. These relate the vicissitudes and achievements of the early pioneers in Eretz-Israel (the Land of Israel), the beauty of the landscape and the revival of the language. Shimoni admires the natural confidence, lost since the days of Isaiah, with which the young children speak Hebrew, "with a fluency unexperienced by Bialik and Yehudah Ha'Levi."

72

A far less sentimental brand of work poetry was offered by Itshak Tavori who chose to take his own life. Like Mikhál and Keats he may be regarded as 'a poet of unfulfilled renown,' as were those cut off in their prime a few years later by the War of Liberation. His attitude to toil is an ambiguous one. A *kibbutz* member himself, he performed his duties well but refused to conform to the parochial tendencies of that remarkable way of life known as 'the collective.' Whatever its merits, for the oversensitive individual it was not the happiest choice:

> 'This boy, have you oft met his like?
> No gusto, no comeliness, haggard and lean.
> But his gaze had the sky to imbibe and its garden to hike,
> And the dew from the herbage of Heaven to glean.
>
> This boy with his wound of a mouth tight and curled —
> Every soft-moulded word was at once furnaced hard.
> At the cliff of your harshness a vessel of daydreams he hurled,
> And his soul and his poetry broke, shard on shard."

(*Tr.* A.B.)

After a backbreaking day of concrete-mixing he proceeds to tell his beloved that, mummified by the terrible heat in the Jordan Valley and crushed by the heavy toil, he has forgotten that day how to love her. Such feelings and attitudes, needless to say, were not welcomed by the more down-to-earth members of the collective and only confirmed their opinion — largely shared by most city-dwellers in those years — that poetry was nothing but 'cosmetics' anyway.

In the mid-thirties the revival of Hebrew was already a *fait accompli*. The old and new concepts, terms and phrases were being fused together with ever increasing intensity, new daily papers sprang up and a healthy, racy *Sabra* slang began to develop. The quality of the spoken and written language, moreover, did not depend on class, education or profession to the extent that it does in Europe or America. At long last the old-new language had come of age, and the new writers were free to devote a larger part of their energies to purely artistic considerations, to bolder techniques and, most important of all, to finding and cultivating their own voice.

Leah Goldberg (1911-) was born in Kovno, Lithuania. Her mother-tongue was Russian and she mastered several languages before learning Hebrew thoroughly. The selection of Hebrew as her medium of expression presented an *embarras de choix* which amounted to a minor crisis. From her youth she has been an ardent Zionist, belonging to the left wing yet maintaining a sound respect for the old traditions. (Very wisely she has left socialism out of her poetry: the two don't mix too well, certainly not under a woman's pen.) She has done important work in many literary fields as essayist, lecturer, editor and translator. At present she holds the chair of Comparative Literature at the Hebrew University of Jerusalem.

Her poetry is somewhat austere, following in the wake of such hypersensitive poets as Avraham Ben-Itzhak and David Fogel rather than sharp-tongued trail-blazers like Shlonsky or colourful bards like Alterman. The foreground of her poetry is modern, in the sense that she is influenced by current ideas and modes of writing and has contributed important innovations of her own; but the background is conventional, nostalgic in a quiet, dignified manner and tied by many strings to the Old World.

The best thing about Leah Goldberg's poetry is that, unlike so many Hebrew and foreign poets in recent times, she has seldom produced a poem that fails to sing. The tone is that of a delicate viola which, though incapable of reaching the dizzy

heights of a violin concerto, gives a more tender and thought-
ful music and has a lingering effect. The combination of direct,
almost primitive feeling and a sophisticated and highly cultured
mind is seen at its deepest level in the sheaf of twelve sonnets,
The Love of Thérèse du Meun. In these sonnets Leah Gold-
berg 'reconstructs,' as it were, some of the irretrievably lost
sonnets of Mme. du Meun, a woman of the French aristocracy
who lived about four hundred years ago and at the age of
forty fell in love with the young Italian tutor of her sons. When
the tutor left her house she burned all the forty-one sonnets she
had dedicated to him and sought the seculsion of a nunnery,
but the memory of her poems lingered on as a legend. Round
these data the modern Hebrew poetess has woven a fabric so
delicate, so full of empathy, that we are inclined to believe she
actually *was* Thérèse du Meun in a former incarnation:

"The raindrop filaments, like strings, close tight
Upon the window-pane. My friend, please kindle
The hearth-fire. Let us sit among the lights
And watch the silhouettes between us dwindle.

How well you fit into the greyish guise
Of rainy days. Your youthfulness is caught then
Against a double light of flame and autumn —
My heart the ardour and my mind the ice."

(*Tr.* A.B.)

Like Bialik, Leah Goldberg reverts time and again to the
scenes of her childhood. But whereas Bialik lays stress on the
brilliance, the splendour and the colourful variety of his child-
hood's sights — which he was sure would reappear to him at the
hour of his death — Leah Goldberg hankers after the quietude,
the languor, even the mustiness against which the older poet
expressed himself so forcibly. Her description of early spring in
Lithuania is a fine example of her 'static' pictures that are more
dynamic than many modernistic feats:

"Humming stillness. April's close.
A pail the well arouses.
On the doorstep in repose
The beggar-woman drowses.

Sallow, dry and dessicate
As mushrooms from the forest,
Slow her bonnet undulates
Above her modest forehead."

(*Early Spring, Tr.* Dov Vardi)

Compared with the Lithuanian landscape and weather, those of Eretz-Israel must have been arid to her delicate senses. About the *khamseen,* that hot eastern desert-wind which can sap the strength of a Hercules, she complains to God, "Your air is sand and mustard," and for a metaphor of similar strength on this subject we have to wait till David Avidan comes along with

"The sun yawned wildly and the whole forlorn city said amen."

In his essay *Leah Goldberg* (*Israel Argossy,* No. 7, Jerusalem, 1960), Ezra Spicehandler points out that her academic activities may endanger the balance between reason and emotion in her poetry:

"Leah Goldberg is, like many modern poets, not merely an educated poetess but an academic one. This is said with due regard to the fact that Israel's academicians are not yet as removed from life's realities as their Continental or American counterparts. Leah Goldberg in particular has spent a large segment of her life in non-academic activities, yet I have no doubt that her appointment to the chair of comparative literature at the Hebrew University has influenced her in the direction of more intellectualized poetry. To be sure, this tendency toward intellectualism has always been present in her poetry, the academic appointment has only tended to emphasize it:

"Indeed the song is a thorn, proud and dry
Naked and abandoned to the burning sun
Now it rhymes with all sorts
Of wisdom which has foregone beauty."

But, aware that the danger is not an overwhelming one, he hastens to add that the poetess' colourful lyricism has not been impaired and that in her more mature poetry there is an ambiguity (or rather a harmony of contrasts, a kind of counterpoint — A.B.) which is "most startling because, even at her deepest moments, her style remains conversational and boldly visual and concrete:

"We who are ill with knowledge
Wise beyond concealing
How does the joy of the bright world
Burst through our heart?
Who seduces us
To touch, to sense, to see?
Ours, ours, ours
Is the honey in the comb.
For me, once again bloom
The tree and the red rose
My happy heart is planted
At the gates of hell."

Shin Shalom (Shalom Shapira) was born in 1905 in Galicia, Poland, and educated in Austria and Germany. In 1922 he settled in Palestine and worked as a teacher, lecturer and editor. At present he resides in Haifa where he is editor of the yearly literary publication *Carmelit*. He has written poems, stories and plays and translated Shakespeare's sonnets into Hebrew.

The greater part of Shin Shalom's poetry is essentially lyrical but a considerable portion of his efforts is devoted, with various degrees of triumph, to cosmic and national themes. His lyricism contains an element of preoccupation with the mystic nucleus of the soul. This tendency to mysticism is best understood in view of the fact that Shin Shalom is of Hassidic stock,* and though he seldom carries his mystical proclivities as far as the Cabbalist poets did, he is always looking for an intuitive, almost occult shortcut to spiritual influences. With true Hassidic spirit, which ascribes superhuman powers to its leaders, Shin Shalom takes his spiritual *alter ego* for granted. Once this has been established the rest follows realistically, just as *The Picture of Dorian Gray* may be regarded as a realistic novel once we have consented to the postulate that the picture is ageing while Dorian remains young. On reading Shin Shalom's poem *To the Enemy* we are not quite sure, in spite of well-meaning efforts to explain him in psychological terms, who this enemy is, but the vagueness of his identity does not detract from the clarity of the situation as a whole:

"I chiselled my days from the tombstone of sorrow,
I dug me a depth to abide there and brood,
But the sound of your footsteps imbues me with horror,
And whining I shrink from your menacing mood."

(Tr. A.B.)

Various attempts have been made to discuss Shin Shalom's poetry in terms of psychoanalysis, but erudite and penetrating as some of them are they hardly do justice to 'the yeasts in the dough' — that element without which the psychological ingredients cannot be incorporated into one organic entity. The psychologist is mainly concerned with the *Nephesh* (roughly translated as 'psyche') which is subject to the same basic rules in all human beings, even in animals from a certain order upwards. The *Neshamáh* (even more roughly translated as 'soul') is something which only man possesses, and a *Neshamáh Yeteráh* ('a rare soul') is that quality which enables a select few to achieve a perfect balance between reason and emotion and transcend the world's vanities and calamities. Only a man with

* See Glossary and General Notes at the end of this volume.

a *Neshamáh Yeteráh* could go to his death as Reb Mendel did, "with his brow wrinkled, a Torah in his arms, all the while trying stubbornly to solve a difficult Talmudic problem that had bothered him all his life."

It is this element that atones for Shin Shalom's effusiveness and saves him from the pitfall of cheap sentimentality. His 'Zionist' poems in which he identifies his ego with that of the nation are written in the best tradition of the Piyyutim, and while their general standard leaves a lot to be desired, there is a Hassidic devotion in them that can bring even a young *Sabra* sceptic to admit in private that there is much more to them than the rhetoric with which he has been stuffed at school:

> "Tonight I wish to move the valleys' dust
> And summit breezes yet unmarred.
> A brother amid brothers surely must
> Remain on guard.
>
> . . . .
>
> Tonight I wish to stand erect, alone,
> When lots are cast upon the steep hill,
> And conquer life — or consecrate my own
> To Israel, my people."
>
> (*Tr.* A.B.)

In his intensely personal poetry, too, this element is seldom missing. A long and moving poem, *Jealousy Scroll*, describes a betrayed husband whose emotions are the same as those of any other man in a similar position, but the way he goes about it is so typically Hassidic as to turn the poem into a unique litany. Perhaps only a man who has seen and heard the cantor at the synagogue whine his supplication before his Maker can plead so futilely with a woman without loss of self-respect:

> "Take a pair of scissors and cut out his name
> From the calendar of nights.
> Summon all the riddles of your femininity
> And perform a miracle

And make a breach in the wall of Time —
Perhaps the laws of Creation will be reversed,
Perhaps there will still be some hope for us.
And if you cannot do this, how can you demand
That I should forget?"

(Tr. A.B.)

At times the poet's exploration takes him outside the world of reality, creating a kind of surrealist existence which, as the younger poet Moshé Dor points out in his short poem *Unicorns*, one is reluctant to trade for the real thing. In his dream, says Shin Shalom, he has dropped a heavy weight on the paw of a cat:

"In a dream none can tell
A man from a cat,
A heart from a weight.
Thus I was:
The weight that fell,
The paw,
The pain,
The pounce into space,
The terrified yell.
In a dream none can tell
A weight from a heart,
A cat from a man."

(Tr. A.B.)

An appreciation of Shin Shalom's poetry for the benefit of those who do not read Hebrew is an even more difficult matter than that of Shneur's. Though an undisputed master of the language, his poetry does not depend like Shlonsky's on linguistic acrobatics and innovations. It is the old-new element, the *Piyyut* quality blended with the modern realistic and surrealistic symbols, that proves so hard to translate and expound.

Shin Shalom's wide gamut of sensitivity and emotional reaction lifts him far above the stature of a *petit-maître*. His attempts to blow the national ram's horn are seldom convincing, but when he sticks to his natural *milieu*, the literary chamber-music, he can play his clarinet with a Hassidic zest and vibrating enthusiasm that remind us of all the ram's horns we have ever heard. His effusive 'publicism' will eventually grow dated while his fine lyrical poetry will outlive, I think, many of those symbolic glossaries with which the modernistic trend is cluttered.

VIII. Nathan Alterman and the Younger Generation

"You can dismiss his biography in a few paragraphs. . . . Anonymity, detachment of his personal self from his poetry, these are ingrained in Nathan Alterman's personality. If he does any grappling with himself, he has kept it pretty well submerged. . . . He sings the on and the about. The world is his object, its stars and its wrongs, its galleries of hate and its crowded tiers cracking peanuts above the arena. Nathan Alterman, the man within the poet, his origins and makings — these have become so completely distilled into his work that they are almost traceless."

These are the opening words of Dov Vardi's essay on Alterman in his book *New Hebrew Poetry* (Tel Aviv, 1947). We have chosen to start this part of the Introduction with Alterman because, although he was not actually born in Eretz-Israel, he is rightly regarded by many as the first *Sabra* poet and his verse is imbued with its landscape and emotional sphere. He was born in Poland in 1910, spent his early childhood in Besserabia (whose colourful surroundings enhanced the 'bardic' element in his poetry), went to Palestine with his family and was one of the first Hebrew writers to graduate from a secondary school there. His agricultural studies in France and subsequent work in Palestine brought him close to the problems of the land and the newly established *Yishuv*, preparing the ground for his heartfelt verse when the great struggle for independence came. He soon turned to literature, participating in various periodicals and contributing to the modern trend started by Shlonsky and Leah Goldberg. He has written poetry, plays, light verse, political and 'occasional' verse — especially his 'seventh column' during the years of national struggle, which boosted public morale as the verses of Sagittarius did during the Battle of Britain — and translated Shakespeare's *The Merry Wives of Windsor* and *The Taming of the Shrew*, Shaw's *Doctor's Dilemma*, Racine's *Phèdre* and many other works of poetry, prose and drama from various languages.

While most Hebrew poets of all generations have sung the wonders of Jerusalem, Alterman is a staunch patriot of the newly founded city of Tel Aviv. By no stretch of imagination can Tel Aviv be called an architectural beauty, but it is the centre of industrial, commercial, bohemian, journalistic and literary life of the country. If Jerusalem with its timeless aura, its religious and traditional halo, its picturesque landscape and its academic centres is the heart of the nation, Tel Aviv may be compared to the liver of the new organism, possessing considerable regenerative powers and throbbing with greyish but energetic creativeness. It is this last trait that Alterman admires most of all and goes to seek in the *parbár*, the industrial suburb which is the antithesis of residential suburbia:

> "O shrill, grimacing, open suburb
> Where horses neigh and bellows bloat,
> Cavorting in the draymen's hubbub
> And singing from the barrels' throats —
>
> . . . .

On hearing your Hebraic scriptures
That juicy mouths so subtly blend,
The lasses' hearts will swell with rapture
And pundits' hairs will stand on end."

                                    (*Tr.* A.B.)

Just as Shneur wrote with admiration about those "healthy, uncouth tradesmen and menial workers that saved the sap and lifeblood of the Jewish people throughout the long exile," so Alterman sings the praises of simple folk and simple toil. His first love for agriculture has been transformed into a deep affection for *Melakháh*, humdrum work which 'the anonymous joy of duty and responsibility' saves from degenerating into slavish or criminal drudgery. In his attitude towards work Alterman differs sharply from his predecessors who have made a cult of it. He does not sing odes *to* it — he sings *about* it like a freethinking troubadour who knows that 'the weakness of the deed from time immemorial is its secret desire to be mentioned in idle song.'

Alterman treats work and nearly all other themes like a true bard — openly blithe or sorrowful, manifestly middle-browed, with an amount of frothiness that makes it hard to know where truth ends and illusion begins. This method reaches an artistic climax in *The Purchase of the Fair*, a long fanciful poem allegedly narrated by Rabba Bar-Bar-Hanna, the Münchhausen of the Talmud. Its hero goes to a country fair with his two 'kiddies' and, seized by a sudden whim, decides to buy the whole fair lock, stock and barrel. A petty-minded moneychanger tries to thwart his plan and is greeted with a torrent of abuse, highly lauded by the author for its artistic merits:

"Long live the art of swearing, bold of nerve and tendon,
Long may its beauties thunder down their mood.
Our speech disrobes in them with sudden, stark abandon
And harems rise, word-harems of the nude.

No platitudes the master of invective burgeons,
No ready-made rejoinders mar his job.
Like sea-shells he selects them, delicate and virgin,
From regions unmolested by the mob."

Our hero wins the two-man auction but when it comes to paying he announces that he hasn't a penny to his name. He then makes a gallant effort to persuade the fair that it should submit to his whim without payment, upsetting the conventional order of things and winning its freedom from the money-changers' bondage:

"Some more light-headedness, some less servility —
Just name your wish and presto! — part and parcel
Of God's own living truth — no mere similitude —
We foster from these mercenary farces.

And lest we miss our joke on such a day convivial,
Why not uproot those orders we contest,
Those calculations of profound oblivion,
And make of *them* an everlasting jest?"

But the improvised entreaties of a man of spirit can hardly convince an enraged mob, and our hero gets a sound drubbing and escapes by the skin of his teeth like Charlie Chaplin in one of his old films:

"A tender hand applies his flannel for a dressing
And both his kiddies limp upon their thigh.
The way is long. Sing, little bird, and shower blessings
On tales you shall continue by-and-by."

(*Tr.* A.B.)

Two Jewish traits are manifest in this picturesque poem. One is the time-honoured readiness to spin a story at a moment's notice, the other a perfect blend of the old and new values. Here as elsewhere the influence of Yiddish folk-elements is strongly felt, though it is modernized to meet the requirements of sophisticated readership.

The best example of these qualities is given in Alterman's crowning achievement, *The Song of Ten Brethren*. Assembled at a country inn the ten brothers are held up for the night by the rising flood. To pass the time each of them 'sings' a song on a different theme: *ars poetica*, wine, family, frivolity, work and so forth. The mainstay of the whole structure is *The Father*, a motive which must have haunted Alterman for quite a long time. After several attempts made elsewhere, which cannot be regarded as entirely felicitous, he has managed to come up with a much finer poem.

> "His leonine shade scales the wall, shade of illness and
>   dungeon,
> But calm is the father, no spring in his step, no rebound.
> All emblems of sadness are vague, flying off at a tangent —
> The sorrow that nears him is thorough, meticulous, bound.
>
> Adroitly it strikes at his innards, a touch of the master,
> A hundred and one apprehensions and Death at the
>   threshold.
> The piecemeal collapse of his body, the crack of its plaster —
> He tenses and marvels, his childlike curiosity freshened."

It is typical of the *Piyyut* tradition that the poem, which begins in a restrained tone, waxes warmer when the flesh-and-blood father is supplanted by a symbolic one, addressed in the second person, and the two merge into a solid entity:

> "The world is your own, is your mansion, the child that you
>   foster,
> Whose illness you carry, whose morrow you shoulder at
>   twilight.
> Its evils you face, through its dragons you walk unaccosted,
> But scamper in fright from the ranters of rhetoric's high-
>   light.

Not yours is the heretic's licence, the spite and derision
That beckon to overripe women and green poetasters;
Not yours is the glee of extremes—*you* were born to
    envisage
The treadmill of people, the highway routine and disasters."

There follows a sustained diminuendo, a short lyrical inter-
lude and towards the end, switching again to the third person,
the poet offers a shorter and more intense Piyyut woven around
the moment of crisis:

"Effaced is this near-timeless ant, this trackless warrior
Who trudges through annals of heartache and malice that
    fester.
Wicks' crackle. Fall's thunderbolts. Sharpshooting anguish.
    Memorial
Of glow and disease, cogitation till morning unrested."

(*Tr.* A.B.)

Alterman's love poems, as well as other manifestations of per-
sonal experience in verse, seldom rise to the level of his indirect
lyricism. Perhaps he is too worldly-wise to play the loving
fool as a poet of love must do from time to time. Perhaps his
smile, like that of *The Father,* is burdened with a look of
sagacity. There are many exquisite lines in his love poetry ('The
silence between heartbeats is yours'). There is a perfect blend
of tone, mood and idea that would have raised more than one
poem to the level of Heine had they been a trifle less com-
placent, a trifle more eager for emotional catharsis. On the
whole — excepting poems like *The Father* and *The Foundling*
and sticking our necks far into the noose of prediction — it would
seem that his bardic, colourful, picaresque verses have the best
chance of standing the test of time. People will always be de-
lighted with Rabba Bar-Bar-Hanna, with the Troubadours and
Minnesingers, with Münchausen and Saroyan. There is in these
poems an innocuous alcoholic element that warms without in-

toxicating and smells and tastes wonderful. It is 'the cock's ancient clarion' blended with the sweetly shrill oboe notes of modern romanticism. Like the would-be buyer of the Fair we are tempted to contest and upset the order of things even at the risk of being flayed mercilessly by the enemies of earthly pleasures — puritanism and hypocrisy. Perhaps it is because of the order of things that we need to apply the drug of dreams to the pain of living, that we consent to be charmed, inebriated, even hoodwinked by Alterman's never-never-land. There are as yet no real pubs in Israel, but we can always patronize the poetic pub set up by the author of *The Song of Ten Brethren,* where we shall sit and sip our drink and whisper without absolute conviction but with utter relish, "There is magic on this man's lips."

We propose to end this Introduction with a short summary of the work and influence of some poets who belong to the younger generation and whose works, in the course of the last twenty years or so, have changed Hebrew poetry almost beyond recognition yet kept faith in their fashion with the old patterns.

The major events which left their indelible mark on the annals of the Jewish race were the Second World War, during which six million Jews were exterminated by the Nazis, and the advent of the State of Israel which was, to a large extent, a direct result of the former occurrence. The first event was too chaotic, too diabolically drastic, to find true artistic expression as yet, and very few attempts to portray it have been included in this anthology.

The second event, essentially positive in spite of the heavy sacrifices involved, gave a new freshness to the writing of a generation brought up in the tense but highly gratifying atmosphere of national struggle, and made it easier for the younger poets to cultivate their own voice, though often at a high price. The remarkable vicissitudes of the *Haganah* (Defence Force) which grew into the Army of Israel, the glorification of its legendary *Palmakh* (Striking Force) — all too often at the expense of other militant and military units — created a certain trend of thought, feeling and behaviour that remained in fashion for well-nigh fifteen years. Its main characteristics were a genuine but tiresome nonchalance, a Sabra frankness of speech and emotion "as direct as the methods of a court reporter and sometimes just as bad," and a spirit of bravado and comradely affection that helped Israel out of many difficulties but gave prominence to a plethora of poetasters. Where a chanting choir carries the day the Muses have a hard time, and only a few of the *Palmakh* poets outgrew their fame to produce satisfactory verse. The best and most lovable of these, Haim Gouri (1923-) has even managed to write some memorable poems about the war and his fallen comrades. Harsh as it may sound, the very fact that the war was *not* fought in vain impairs the poetic value of such verses: in a war for survival and independence there is no place for the superb irony and self-mockery bred by a purposeless struggle.

Gouri's fine lyrical poetry reaches a higher level, and it is most refreshing to recall that the person who has paid such a heavy toll to military and public affairs as a fighter and journalist can write so quietly and convincingly about stalactites and stalagmites:

> "Stone-flowers stare opaquely at the ceiling
> And shimmer in the darkness, droplet-born,
> Against the light that walks on all-fours, stealing
> Through manikins of moss and tangled fern."
>
> (*In the Cave, Tr.* A.B.)

The last fifteen years have witnessed the ever-increasing influence of English and American poetry on contemporary Israeli writers. Various factors, notably the ties with the United States and the heritage of the British mandate in Palestine — a positive one insofar as the English language is concerned — have brought

Israel into the 'Anglo-Saxon cultural sphere.' Today most of the country's intelligentsia read English fluently and some writers even express themselves in this language and translate their own and other works from the Hebrew.

In the 1950's Hebrew poetry was still influenced by French and German writers, especially Valéry and Rilke, but these influences have been gradually supplanted by those of W. B. Yeats, T. S. Eliot, Ezra Pound, W. H. Auden and, to a lesser extent, E. E. Cummings. It must be remembered that these poets, particularly Eliot and Pound, were influenced in turn by Biblical literature. True to a long tradition fostered by its close proximity to Aramaic, Greek, Latin, Arabic, German, French and Russian, the old-new Hebrew tongue now throve under the impact of English, absorbing many new ingredients but maintaining its own character under a pressure that would have crushed a weaker language.

A good example of a young writer whose poetic personality remains unimpaired in spite of German and English influences is given by the work of Dan Paggis (1930-   ) who has the gift of making abstract or impersonal entities come alive:

"At an hour of perspicuity he traced
as in an alchemist's pellucid phial
the transmutations of his body. In his veins
a fiery quicksilver throbbed. He forced
his glance to penetrate the hiding-place
where, like a spider in its web, surprised,
his heart hung in the balance."
(*The Experiment, Tr.* A.B.)

Like so many of his contemporaries, Paggis often treats Biblical themes from a modern point of view. When the Flood was over, says he, and the survivors burst forth from Noah's Ark and gave vent to their pent-up emotions,

> "... it was the end
> For those prehensile, carefree fish, they who had thriven
> Upon the tragedy, quick-witted profiteers
> Who now were trapped in a congealing earth
> And, lashing tail and fin,
> With mouths agape, were drowning in the air."
>
> (*Ararat*, Tr. A.B.)

Biblical themes, suffused with the spirit of the Aggadah, also abound in the work of Yehudah Amikhai (1924-   ), a poet of considerable communicative powers. The mixture of modernism and romanticism in his poems has the knack of making new symbols seem ancient and time-old notions seem ultra-modernistic. The reader may recall a visual quiz published a few years ago in an American magazine, where very ancient and very modern pieces of sculpture were shown together and one had to tell them apart. Had such a test been devised in the field of poetry we would have had a hard time with some of Amikhai's poems. His long poem *The Visit of the Queen of Sheba* can serve as an example of this perfect fusion of the old and new, achieved by Amikhai's peculiar technique of pouring old wine into new vessels and new wine into old ones. The famous visit to King Solomon is described not as a feast of reason but as an orgy of wild instincts, and once these have been satisfied the whole paraphernalia of wisdom — riddles, parables, metaphors and so forth — is of no earthly use:

> "Sawdust of quizzes,
> nutshells of parables,
> woolly stuffing for
> delicate riddles.
>
> Coarse burlap for
> love and contrivance.
> Cast-off conundrums
> rustling in the litter."
>
> (*Tr.* A.B.)

In a brilliant poem like this, Amikhai can exercise to the full his gift of coining succinct imagery and applying it in the right place. In his lyrical poetry, however, we sometimes have the feeling that the poet should have practised a little more austerity. *To the Woman,* for instance, opens with a prolific display of similes and metaphors that becomes emotionally stirring only towards the end:

> "Your right hand is dangling from your dream.
> Your hair is memorizing its nightly lesson
> From the wind's tattered textbook.
> . . . .
> When you open your coat
> I have to double my love.
> . . . .
> When you are smiling
> All serious notions grow tired."

Austerity carried to its ultimate extreme typifies some of the poetry written by Nathan Zakh (1930-   ). His short, highly concentrated poem about the last days of King Saul employs an original technique which proves poignantly how much of a neurotic Saul was ever since he had had a premonition that his days were numbered:

> "For Saul listens to Music.
> Is this the Music
> Saul should listen to
> As times go?
> Yes, this is the Music that Saul
> Should listen to as times go
> For there is no other now
> And perhaps there will be none
> Till Mount Gilboa."

>   (*Tr.* Meir Wieseltier)

Here total austerity is a 'must' and any unbending towards romanticism would ruin the whole poem. In other places, however, Zakh is confronted by the same danger which Hemingway encounters in his short stories, namely, that toughness carried too far is just an inversion of sentimentality. Perhaps the right way to avoid an overdose is to remember that austerity, like a gentleman's mistakes, should never be committed unwittingly.

In another poem, depicting a different kind of neurotic — a man haunted not by the sense of inevitable disaster but by a chronic capacity for unhappiness — the almost monastic austerity has an intense effect:

> "From year to year this gets more subtle,
> It will be so subtle in the end, —
> She said, meaning just this.
>
> But time and again I can feel I am drowning in Time,
> I feel I have been drowning a long time.
> He stopped."

(Tr. Richard Flint)

It is in such poems that the real value of Zakh's work lies, rather than in the slightly heavy-handed romanticism which avoids the linguistic rhetoric so prevalent in his predecessors' verse but substitutes for it a psychological rhetoric that can be quite as dangerous.

This danger is even more keenly felt in the work of David Avidan (1934-) whose poems are nearly always a gamble for all or nothing. With an amount of toughness worthy of a Spanish conquistador and an almost telepathic sensitivity that the Inca priests are said to have possessed, Avidan gave Hebrew poetry a long-overdue shock treatment. While the shriek that went up to the sky ten years ago at the appearance of his first book of poetry has since been considerably mitigated, his poems continue to startle all kinds of prudes, purists and conventionalists.

> ". . . .You're a kitten, a little kitten, a wet
> little witch riding on a hoover toward highflown windows,
>   blending
> delectable poisons under picturesque awnings, purring
> charming refusals in a low engine-lingo, remembering
> the date of payment.
> I could of course put you up, warm you
> with an electric heater, dry you up
> against my thermostatic body, bestow on you
> a gradual, meticulous happiness. . . ."
>
> *(A Clean Miss, Tr. A.B.)*

Avidan's poetry is a true continuation of 'the style of the Big I' initiated by Ibn-Gabirol and developed by Shneur. Recently, however, he has come to realize that his compassion is not quite on a par with his intellect and technique and has tried to make up the deficiency. The best result of his recanting mood is a touching poem called *Kas Buvo — Tai Nebus*, a Lithuanian proverb which means 'what has happened will never happen again':

> "Two ex-Lithuanians, who remember
> their mother-tongue even more vaguely
> than they remember their mothers, meet
> in a café on a fine cool evening and exchange
> memories. Say, how do you say 'past' in Lithuanian?
>   Indeed,
> how do you say it? Embarrassing. Pretty embarrassing.
>   Perhaps
> there is someone in this pleasing area, within
> a radius of two miles or so, who can
> fix this trying lingual short-circuit. But
> it gets very late, and all those Lithuanians
>   who aren't dead yet will be fast asleep.
>
> How do you say 'sleep' in Lithuanian?"
>
> *(Tr. by the author)*

But the majority of Avidan's poems are still launched on a grand scale. His preoccupation with the ionosphere of literature is fully conscious, and his high-octane metaphors are typical of the space age to which he is manifestly proud to belong. Even his iconoclasm follows a similar pattern. He does not break idols — he sends them hurtling into space yet often wishes with a nostalgic sigh that they would return as comets.

Between them Nathan Zakh and David Avidan have done a very creditable job. They cleared away the woolliness, the stagnant parochiality, the stuffy bucolic style that threatened to clog up many literary pathways. They galvanized Hebrew poetry into action, completed the process of urbanization initiated by Alterman, and at their best made one word do the work of ten. Perhaps their greatest victory has been achieved in their vindication of the faith, shared by many modernists all over the world, that this can be done without undue loss of compassion and human understanding.

We have come to the end of our three thousand years' journey. What route will the forthcoming generations follow? Will they continue the fusion of old and new concepts, or will the yearnings for 'normalcy' prevail and make them ignore the past or even be ashamed of it? Will an Israeli boy or girl a few hundred years hence be able to read the literature of our generation with the same facility as we read the Bible and the Aggadah, or will such a task necessitate elaborate preparations similar to those which modern Greek youngsters require if they want to study Homer?

It is my sincere hope that no such wall will rise between the reader of the future and the treasure-house of the past, that writers of Hebrew will always be equally well-versed in the ancient and up-to-date strata of their language and literature, like some present-day skippers whose ships are equipped with radar and other modern devices but who do not fail to watch the flight of birds as their ancestors did thousands of years ago.

Perhaps — and this is one of those things which the heart hardly dares reveal to the mouth — the unique example offered by the revival of the Hebrew language and literature may prompt other cultures to re-examine their own past more closely and realize that nothing is hopelessly archaic, that many values can and should be brought back to life under suitable circumstances. If the present anthology can help towards the attainment of such a goal, the editor will have been amply rewarded.

Hayyim Nahman Bialik
(1873-1934)

LOGOS

Scatter the ember from your altar, Prophet,
And cast it among rogues —
Let them use it for their roasts, to void their pots
To warm their hands.
Cast forth the spark that lingers in your heart
And let them light the cigarette in their mouths,
Illuminate the lurking, evil smile
That cowers thief-like on their hairy lips,
The malice in their eyes.
See how they go, the rascals, how they come,
The prayer that you taught them ever on their lips
Suffering your pain and hoping with your hope
While yet their soul yearns to destroy your altar,
Fall on its ruins, burrow in the heap
Of its remains, tear out the shattered stones
And use them in their thresholds and their walls
And raise them over graves;
And if they find among them your charred heart —
They throw it to their dogs.

Spurn then your altar with contemptuous foot
And let it crumble with its fire and smoke.
Wipe with one stroke the clustered spiders' webs
Tautened to harp-strings in your heart
And weave from them a song of resurrection
Vision of grace — vain prophecy and lies —
Cast them to the wind and let them float away,
Pale shreds in the world's void
On a clear day at summer's end.
No silver strand shall find its friend, no thread
Its mate; they shall be lost in the first squall.
Your hammer, the iron hammer that is broken
From useless striking on their hearts of stone
Break into fragments, beat into a spade
And dig us a grave.
Speak what God's anger puts in your mouth
And let your lips not fear.
Though your word be bitter as death, though it be death
    itself,
Still we shall hear.
See, teeming night enfolds, the shades enclose us
And like blind men we grope.
Something has happened amidst us, none knows what,
None sees or tells,
Whether the sun shone on us or has set,
Or has set for ever.
Great is the chaos all around, and fearful
And there is no refuge.
What though we cry in darkness and we pray —
Who will hear?
And if we utter the cruel curse of God —
On whose head shall it fall?
If we bare our teeth and clench the fist of wrath —
Where falls the blow?
Chaos shall swallow all, the wind shall bear them,

They shall be lost.
There is no staff, no power and no path —
Heaven is silent.
They know their sin against us, their mortal sin —
They bear their guilt in silence.
Open then your mouth and speak, prophet of doom,
If word there be — speak!
Shall we fear death? Its angel rides our backs,
Its bridle in our mouths.
With paeans of revival on our lips, with merry laughter
We hop into the grave.

(Tr. Bernard Lewis)

SUMMER IS DYING

Summer is dying, woven in fine gold,
   Couched on a purple bed
Of falling garden leaves and twilight clouds
   That lave their hearts in red.

The garden is deserted, save where a youth
   Saunters, or a maiden walks,
Casting an eye and a sigh after the flight
   Of the last and lingering storks.

The heart is orphaned. Soon a rainy day
   Will softly tap the pane.
'Look to your boots, patch up your coats, go fetch
   The potatoes in again.'

(Tr. L. V. Snowman)

ON MY RETURN

Here again is the wizened man
   With shrunk and shrivelled look,
Shade of dry stubble, wandering leaf
   That strays from book to book.

Here again is the wizened hag,
  Knitting socks and fumbling,
Her mouth with oaths and curses filled,
  Her lips for ever mumbling.

Our cat is there: he has not stirred
  From his quarters in the house,
But in his oven dream he makes
  A treaty with a mouse.

The rows of spiders' webs are there,
  As of old in darkness, spread
In the western corner, choked with flies,
  Their bodies blown out, dead.

You have not changed, you're antic old,
  There's nothing new I think;
Friends, let me join your club, we'll rot
  Together till we stink.

(Tr. L. V. Snowman)

GOD GRANT MY PART AND PORTION BE . . .

Meek of the earth, humble in wit and works,
Unknown and unseen dreamers, mute of soul,
Stinted in speech, of beauty most abundant,
Privily embroidering your lives —
God grant my part and portion be with you.

Like coral of the reaches of the sea
The pleasant savour of your minds lies hidden
And blooms your nobleness like berries wild
Burgeoning in the shadow of a wood.

Unbidden you are bountiful; and lavish
Without a knowledge of munificence.
O poets of most lovely silence, priests
Amidst the hush and quiet of the Lord,

No alien eye beholds your festivals
No, nor the days of mourning that are yours.
The mighty and the mean, the saint and sinner
You greet without knee-crooking, with the same
Compassionate and comprehending smile.

Tiptoeing slowly through the paths of life,
The heart awake, the ear alert, the eye
Most watchful, for its very touch you shudder
For beauty's least caress, you quake and tremble.
You pass, and without pose or effort sow
That faith and purity that from you flows
Like azure from the dome of heaven, like
Numberless shadows from the pleasant wood.

Yes, skilled in silence, voiceless, without speech,
Utters your mouth no arrogance, your hand
Fashions no masterpieces, works of pride.
Desire and longing do within you fail.
Your place is not with the array of seers,
Nor in museums is your share and lot.
Lonely and echoless your footstep dies.

Howbeit, your life, the simple days of your life —
Behold the vision superb, the work of art,
Ye keepers of God's image up on earth!
Daily, and in the brilliance of your eyes
Yea, in the wrinkles of your countenance
The beauty of your lives does drop by drop
Flow into the hollow of the world
As flows into the river's brimming heart
The waters of a secret spring, unknown.

As the Lord liveth, they will not be lost!
Not the mere flutter of your eyelash, nor
The least accounted stirrings in your heart.
But like the music of the spheres, they will
Forever tremble in the vaulted sky

And even at the end of days, when no
Echo will be of Heimán and Jeduthún,
Nor memory of the wisdom of these two:
Chalcól and Dardá, sages of the east,
Even then these will still live and be revealed
In the light and brilliance of some unknown's gaze
Or in the wrinkles of his countenance.

(*Tr.* A. M. Klein)

WHENCE AND WHITHER
(folk song, abridged)

Whence and Whither?
We had no inkling,
But the eyes that saw her,
She set them twinkling.

Lightsome and lively,
She went up and down
And set in commotion
The whole of our town.

That day or that night
As she walked in the street
The youth of our town
Fell flat at her feet.

That day or that night
In every house,
A bickering started
'Twixt man and spouse.

Good women whispered
O'er knitting pins,
Old men winked slyly
And scratched their chins.

Then one day she vanished
Without a 'goodbye' . . .
No one knew whither
And no one knew why.

The laughter was hushed,
The wood was neglected:
There was no one in it.
And no one expected.

As on dull grey days
That come out of season,
All went depressed
And knew not the reason.

The boys came home punctual,
All meek and mild,
Bride and bridegroom
Were reconciled.

Young husbands sit
And yawn with their wives,
Who were never so loving
In all their lives.

No fun in the dark,
In the lane no delight —
Father and mother
Can sleep all night.

No quarrels, no shouts,
And nothing unlawful.
Peace in and peace out —
And the dullness is awful!

          (*Tr.* Helena Frank)

LO BAYOM VE 'LO BALAYLA
(folk song)

Neither daily neither nightly
Through the fields I wander lightly.

Not in Europe nor in Asia
Out there stands an old acacia.

This acacia I importune:
Thorny One, do tell my fortune.

Answer me and do not tarry —
Who's the one I'm gonna marry?

From the highland or the lowland?
Lithuania or Poland?

Is he rich, equipped with carriage,
Or the poorest of the parish?

And a brooch, a little trinket,
Or a necklace, will he bring it?

His hair, is it thin or rippling?
Is he widowed or a stripling?

Or an old man? Then I'd rather
Die, and so I'll tell my father:

'Though my thread of life you sever
I shan't take an old man — never!'

I'll shriek like a wounded starling,
'Not a greybeard, Poppa darling!'
(Tr. A.B.*)*

THE CITY OF SLAUGHTER
(from *Songs of Wrath*)

Arise and go now to the city of slaughter;
Into its courtyard wind thy way.
There with thine own hand touch, an˙ with the eyes of
    thine head
Behold on tree, on stone, on fence, on mural clay,
The spattered blood and dried brains of the dead.
Proceed then to the ruins, the split walls reach,
Where wider grows the hollow and greater grows the
    breach;
Pass over the shattered hearth, attain the broken wall
Whose burnt and barren brick, whose charred stones reveal
The open mouths of such wounds, that no mending
Shall ever mend, nor healing ever heal.
There will thy feet in feathers sink, and stumble
On wreckage doubly wrecked, scroll heaped on manuscript,
Fragments again fragmented —
Pause not upon this havoc; go thy way.
The perfumes will be wafted from the acacia bud
And half its blossoms will be feathers,
Whose smell is the smell of blood!
And, spiting thee, strange incense they will bring —
Banish thy loathing—all the beauty of the spring,
The thousand golden arrows of the sun,
Will flash upon thy malison;
The sevenfold rays of broken glass
Over thy sorrow joyously will pass,
For God called up the slaughter and the spring together:
The slayer slew, the blossom burst, and it was sunny
    weather!
Then wilt thou flee to a yard, observe its mound.
Upon the mound lie two, and both are headless —
A Jew and his hound.
The self-same axe struck both, and both were flung

Unto the self-same heap where swine seek dung;
Tomorrow the rain will wash their mingled blood
Into the runnels, and it will be lost
In rubbish heap, in stagnant pool, in mud.
Its cry will not be heard.
It will descend into the deep, or water the cockle-burr,
And all things will be as they ever were.

Unto the attic mount, upon thy feet and hands;
Behold the shadow of death among the shadows stands.
There in the dismal corner, there in the shadowy nook,
Multitudinous eyes will look
Upon thee from the sombre silence —
The spirits of the martyrs are these souls,
Gathered together, at long last,
Beneath these rafters and in these ignoble holes.
The hatchet found them here, and hither do they come
To seal with a last look, as with their final breath,
The agony of their lives, the terror of their death.
Tumbling and stumbling wraiths, they come, and cower
    there.
Their silence whimpers, and it is their eyes which cry
Wherefore, O Lord, and why?
It is a silence only God can bear.
Lift then thine eyes to the roof; there's nothing there
Save silences that hang from rafters
And brood upon the air:
Question the spider in his lair!
His eyes beheld these things; and with his web he can
A tale unfold, horrific to the ear of man:
A tale of cloven belly, feather-filled;
Of nostrils nailed, of skull-bones bashed and spilled;
Of murdered men who from the beams were hung,
And of a babe beside its mother flung,
His mother speared, the poor chick finding rest
Upon its mother's cold and milkless breast;

Of how a dagger halved an infant's word,
Its 'ma' was heard, its 'mama' never heard.
O, even now its eyes from me demand accounting,
For these the tales the spider is recounting,
Tales that do puncture the brain, such tales that sever
Thy body, spirit, soul from life, forever!
Then wilt thou bid thy spirit: — *Hold, enough!*
Stifle the wrath that mounts within thy throat,
Bury these things accursed,
Within the depth of thy heart, before thy heart will burst!
Then wilt thou leave that place, and go thy way —
And lo! — the earth is as it was, the sun still shines;
It is a day like any other day.

Descend then to the cellars of the town,
There where the virgin daughters of thy folk were fouled,
Where seven heathen flung a woman down,
The daughter in the presence of her mother,
The mother in the presence of her daughter,
Before slaughter, during slaughter and after slaughter!
Touch with thy hand the cushion stained; touch
The pillow incarnadined:
This is the place the wild ones of the wood, the beasts of
    the field
With bloody axes in their paws compelled thy daughters to
    yield:
Beasted and swined!
Note also, do not fail to note,
In that dark corner and behind that cask
Crouched husbands, bridegrooms, brothers, peering from
    the cracks,
Watching the martyred bodies struggling underneath
The bestial breath,
Stifled in filth, and swallowing their blood.
Watching from the darkness and its mesh
The lecherous rabble portioning for booty

Their kindred and their flesh.
Crushed in their shame, they saw it all;
They did not stir or move;
They did not pluck their eyes out, they
Beat not their brains against the wall,
Perhaps, perhaps, each watcher had it in his heart to pray,
A miracle, O Lord, and spare my skin this day!
Those who survived this foulness, who from their blood
    awoke,
Beheld their life polluted, the light of their world gone out —
How did their menfolk bear it, how did they bear this yoke?
They crawled forth from their holes and fled to the house of
    the Lord,
They offered thanks to Him, the sweet benedictory word.
The *Cohanim* sallied forth, to the Rabbi's house they flitted:
Tell me, O Rabbi, tell, is my own wife permitted?
And thus the matter ends, and nothing more;
And all is as it was before.

Come, now, and I will bring thee to their lairs
The privies, jakes and pigpens where the heirs
Of Hasmoneans lay, with trembling knees,
Concealed and cowering, — the sons of the Maccabees!
The seed of saints, the scions of the lions . . .
Who, crammed by scores in all the sanctuaries of their
    shame,
So sanctified My name!
It was the flight of mice they fled
The scurrying of roaches was their flight;
They died like dogs, and they were dead!
And on the next morn, after the terrible night
The son who was not murdered found
The spurned cadaver of his father on the ground.
Now wherefore dost thou weep, O son of man?

Descend into the valley; verdant, there

A garden flourishes, and in the garden
A barn, a shed, — it was their abattoir;
There, like a host of vampires, puffed and bloated,
Besotted with blood, swilled from the scattered dead,
The tumbril wheels lie spread —
Their open spokes, like fingers stretched for murder,
Like vampire-mouths their hubs still clotted red.
Enter not now, but when the sun descends
Wrapt in bleeding clouds and girt with flame,
Then open the gate and stealthily do set
Thy foot within the ambient of horror:
Terror floating near the rafters, terror
Against the walls in darkness hiding,
Terror through the silence sliding.
Didst thou not hear beneath the heap of wheels
A stirring of crushed limbs? Broken and racked
Their bodies move a hub, a spoke
Of the circular yoke;
In death-throes they contort,
In blood disport;
And their last groaning, inarticulate
Rises above thy head,
And it would seem some speechless sorrow,
Sorrow infinite,
Is prisoned in this shed.
It is, it is the Spirit of Anguish!
Much-suffering and tribulation-tried
Which in this house of bondage binds itself.
It will not ever from its pain be pried.
Brief-weary and forespent, a dark Shekhinah
Runs to each nook and cannot find its rest;
Wishes to weep, but weeping does not come;
Would roar, is dumb.
Its head beneath its wing, its wing outspread
Over the shadows of the martyred dead,

Its tears in dimness and in silence shed.
And thou, too, son of man, close now the gate behind thee;
Be closed in darkness now; now thine that charnel space;
So tarrying there thou wilt be one with pain and anguish
And wilt fill up with sorrow thine heart for all its days.
Then on the day of thine own desolation
A refuge will it seem, —
Lying in thee like a curse, a demon's ambush,
The haunting of an evil dream,
O, carrying it in thy heart, across the world's expanse
Thou wouldst proclaim it, speak it out, —
But thy lips shall not find its utterance.

Beyond the suburbs go, and reach the burial ground.
Let no man see thy going; attain that place alone,
A place of sainted graves and martyr-stone.
Stand on the fresh-turned soil.
Such silence will take hold of thee, thy heart will fail
With pain and shame, yet I
Will let no tear fall from thine eye.
Though thou wilt long to bellow like the driven ox
That bellows, and before the altar balks,
I will make hard thy heart, yea, I
Will not permit a sigh.
See, see, the slaughtered calves, so smitten and so laid;
Is there a price for their death? How shall that price be
    paid?
Forgive, ye shamed of the earth, yours is a pauper-Lord —
Poor was He during your life, and poorer still of late.
When to my door you come to ask for your reward,
I'll open wide: see, I am fallen from my high estate.
I grieve for you, my children, my heart is sad for you.
Your dead were vainly dead; and neither I nor you
Know why you died or wherefore, for whom, nor by what
    laws;

Your deaths are without reason; your lives are without cause.
What says the Shekhinah? In the clouds it hides
In shame, in agony alone abides;
I, too, at night, will venture on the tombs,
Regard the dead and weigh their secret shame,
But never shed a tear, I swear it in My name.
For great is the anguish, great the shame on the brow;
But which is greater, son of man, say thou —
Or liefer keep thy silence, bear witness in My name
To the hour of My sorrow, the moment of My shame.
And when thou dost return
Bring thou the blot of My disgrace upon thy people's head,
And from My suffering do not part,
But set it like a stone within their heart.

Turn, then, to leave the cemetery ground,
And for a moment thy swift eye will pass
Upon the verdant carpet of the grass —
A lovely thing! Fragrant and moist, as it is always at the
    coming of the Spring.
The stubble of death, the growth of tombstones!
Take thou a fistful, fling it on the plain
Saying, "the people is plucked grass; can plucked grass grow
    again?"
Turn then thy gaze from the dead, and I will lead
Thee from the graveyard to thy living brothers,
And thou wilt come, with those of thine own breed,
Into the synagogue, and on a day of fasting,
To hear the cry of their agony, their weeping everlasting.
Thy skin will grow cold, the hair on thy skin stand up,
And thou wilt be by fear and trembling tossed;
Thus groans a people which is lost.
Look in their hearts, behold a dreary waste,
Where even vengeance can revive no growth,
And yet upon their lips no mighty malediction

Rises, no blasphemous oath.
Are they not real, their bruises?
Why is their prayer false?
Why, in the day of their trials
Approach me with pious ruses,
Afflict me with denials?
Regard them now, in these their woes:
Ululating, lachrymose,
Crying from their throes,
We have sinned! and *Sinned have we!* —
Self-flagellative with confession's whips.
Their hearts, however, do not believe their lips.
Is it, then, possible for shattered limbs to sin?
Wherefore their cries imploring, their supplicating din?
Speak to them, bid them rage!
Let them against me raise the outraged hand, —
Let them demand!
Demand the retribution for the shamed
Of all the centuries and every age!
Let fists be flung like stone
Against the heavens and the heavenly Throne!

And thou too, son of man, be part of these:
Believe the pangs of their heart, believe not their litanies.
And when the cantor lifts his voice to cry:
Remember the martyrs, Lord,
Remember the cloven infants, Lord,
Consider the sucklings, Lord,
And when the pillars of the synagogue shall crack at this
      piteous word
And terror shall take thee, fling thee in its deep,
Then I will harden My heart; I will not let thee weep.
Should then a cry escape from thee,
I'll stifle it within thy throat.
Let them assoil their tragedy,

Not thou — let it remain unmourned
For distant ages, times remote,
But thy tear, son of man, remain unshed!
Build thou about it, with thy deadly hate
Thy fury and thy rage, unuttered,
A wall of copper, the bronze triple plate!
So in thy heart it shall remain confined
A serpent in its nest — O terrible tear! —
Until by thirst and hunger it shall find
A breaking of its bond. Then shall it rear
Its venomous head, its poisoned fangs, and wait
To strike the people of thy love and hate!

Leave now this place at twilight to return
And to behold these creatures who arose
In terror at dawn, at dusk now, drowsing, worn
With weeping, broken in spirit, in darkness shut.
Their lips still move with words unspoken.
Their hearts are broken.
No lustre in the eye, no hoping in the mind,
They grope to seek support they shall not find:
Thus when the oil is gone the wick still sends its smoke;
Thus does an old beast of burden still bear its yoke.
Would that misfortune had left them some small solace
Sustaining the soul, consoling their gray hairs!
Behold, the fast is ended; the final prayers are said.
But why do they tarry now, these mournful congregations?
Shall it be also read,
The Book of Lamentations?
It is a preacher mounts the pulpit now.
He opens his mouth, he stutters, stammers. Hark
The empty verses from his speaking flow.
And not a single mighty word is heard
To kindle in the hearts a single spark.
The old attend his doctrine, and they nod.

The young ones hearken to his speech; they yawn.
The mark of death is on their brows; their God
Has utterly forsaken every one.

And thou, too, pity them not, nor touch their wound;
Within their cup no further measure pour.
Wherever thou wilt touch, a bruise is found.
Their flesh is wholly sore.
For since they have met pain with resignation
And have made peace with shame,
What shall avail thy consolation?
They are too wretched to evoke thy scorn.
They are too lost thy pity to evoke.
So let them go, then, men to sorrow born,
Mournful and slinking, crushed beneath their yoke.
Go to their homes, and to their hearth depart —
Rot in the bones, corruption in the heart.
And when thou shalt rise upon the morrow
And go upon the highway,
Thou shalt then meet these men destroyed by sorrow,
Sighing and groaning, at the doors of the wealthy,
Proclaiming their sores like so much peddler's wares,
The one his battered head, the other his limbs unhealthy,
One shows a wounded arm, and one a fracture bares.
And all have eyes that are the eyes of slaves,
Slaves flogged before their masters;
And each one begs, and each one craves:
Reward me, Master, for that my skull is broken,
Reward me for my father who was martyred!
The rich ones, all compassion, for the pleas so bartered
Extend them staff and bandage, say 'good riddance' and
The tale is told:
The paupers are consoled.

Away, you beggars, to the charnel-house!
The bones of your fathers disinter!

Cram them into your knapsacks, bear
Them on your shoulders, and go forth
To do your business with these precious wares
At all the country fairs!
Stop on the highway, near some populous city,
And spread on your filthy rags
Those martyred bones that issue from your bags,
And sing, with raucous voice, your pauper's ditty.
So will you conjure up the pity of the nations,
And so *their* sympathy implore.
For you are now as you have been of yore
And as you stretched your hand so you will stretch it,
And as you have been wretched so are you wretched.

What is thy business here, O son of man?
Rise, to the desert flee!
The cup of affliction thither bear with thee!
Take thou thy soul, rend it in many a shred,
With impotent rage, thy heart deform,
Thy tear upon the barren boulders shed,
And send thy bitter cry into the storm!

(*Tr.* A. M. Klein)

SHOULD I BE A RABBI?

Should I be a rabbi?
Haven't got the learning.
Shall I go in business?
Not on what I'm earning!

O my luck is very bad,
I am neither this nor that.
Whither shall I go and why?
What am I and who am I?

Library
Brevard Junior College
Cocoa, Florida

In my pockets not a dime
Now or any other time;
In my hayloft stands no hay,
Horse has croaked and groom's away.
Whistle's dry, and got no liquor,
Wife's a regular Yom Kippur;
Sitting on a boulder stone
I cry bitterly, alone.

Should I be a tailor?
Haven't got the thread.
Possibly a gravedigger?
I'm timid with the dead.

O my luck etc.

What about a bartender?
Where's my beer to hustle?
Shall I be a drayman?
Never had the muscle.

O my luck etc.

What about an innkeeper?
My house isn't built yet.
Should I seek a dowry?
My wife isn't killed yet.

O my luck etc.

Weaver? Where does wool and flax
Grow so I could pick it?
Should I win the lottery?
Haven't bought a ticket.

O my luck etc.

Should I be a jester?
My heart's no longer in it.
What about a highwayman?
They'd hang me in a minute.

O my luck etc.

Shohet? Knife might cut me,
How can I consider it?
Should I be a schoolteacher?
Woe's me, I'm illiterate.

                                        O my luck etc.

Shoemaker? My awl is blunt,
That's not what my job is.
Should I be an engineer?
I won't ride on *Shabbes.*

                                        O my luck etc.

Plumber? I know nothing of
Piping, more's the pity.
Should I be a wet-nurse?
Haven't got the titty.

                                        O my luck etc.
                                    (*Tr.* Grace Goldin)

PROPHET, GO FLEE THEE AWAY

> *"Also Amaziah, priest of Bethel,*
> *said unto Amos, O thou seer, go*
> *flee thee away."*
>
> (*Amos* 7:12)

Go flee? Not I who slowly stalk
The silent cows in rural tracks.
My tongue is dumb to finer talk
And tumbles like a heavy axe.

And not my strength but yours that broke
Is due for blame in aught I failed:
No anvil met my sturdy stroke
And rotten wood my blows assailed.

But why lament? I quit this toil,
Resign to Fate, collect my tools,

And, stripped of fruitless labour's spoils,
Shall vanish from the sight of fools.

To sycamores I shall retire,
To sunny valleys, safe and warm.
And you, you sons of muck and mire,
Tomorrow shall be swept by storm.

(*Tr.* A.B.)

Saul Tchernikhovsky (1875-1943)

ON THE BLOOD
(A Cycle of Sonnets)

I

Tired of mankind, the ages' legacy
Bearing a paltry and an emptied heart,
Devoid of strength and will, each man apart,
We stumble like a horse that cannot see.

We float on rafts swept by a stormy sea,
Like addicts deadened by the poppy's art;
Each jealous of his fledgeling lest it start
To look towards the light and to be free.

God's lightnings rend the skies from side to side,
Piercing the clouds — and if the petty sight
Sees it at all, 'tis as a tiny spark —

Thus do we stare at Genesis, squint-eyed:
In webs of mystery, rotting in the dark,
Our eyes are yearning for the distant light.

II

Our eyes are yearning for the distant light:
But codes of stupid, miming apes oppress
Our hearts, o'erburdened with the pettiness
Of dull and empty days, trivial and trite,

As in the days when we were young and bright,
Dandled by nurses who with tenderness
Re-echoed tales of vaunting wickedness,
Of holy martyrs, suffering for the right.

A mushroom doctrine springs up overnight,
With soldiers' curse and drivers' jest it brings
From ant-like minds, a host of verdant things.

That in the scales their thousand sins outweigh.
Renewing faith, a faith that passed away;
Ageing, we wait the great and wondrous sight.

III

Ageing, we wait the great and wondrous sight —
O simple childish heart who sowed that seed
Of mercy, duty, love — a fatal creed —
Who drew those heart-strings, sensitive and slight?

Sensitive strings! Songs there are, clear and bright —
But shamed by man, through hunger or through greed. . .
— Salvation is not near — men do not heed
Mid hucksters' haggling and the cossacks' spite.

The lustres of the heavenly host abate,
On earth the mighty evil holds its sway,
Though you have saved your soul, your wound is great,

Yours still the vision, far from treachery . . .
When ends the dream — forever? — or a day? —
We rove and seek for creeds and mystery.

IV

We rove and seek for creeds and mystery,
Bald-pated or long-haired, in sombre guise,
While moonstruck loons with epileptic cries
Lead and mislead and trade in ecstasy.

Dark is the fog of time and history,
And like a blazing sun it blinds our eyes;
While stagnant waters whence foul vapours rise,
Fuse hearts to harps with monstrous alchemy.

Our soul is sick and we are sore oppressed
With seeking, and the flame of beacons bright
Bequeathed by men inspired on a great quest.

And like the chaff outside the granary
We flaunt a barren thought, we are too light,
We turn to streams, and paths of fantasy . . .

V

We turn to streams, and paths of fantasy . . .
With scattered crumbs and with the bread of scorn
We bow and scrape with flattering lips and fawn
On world reformers, turning history

To wondrous buildings, drowning misery.
Yet when they rise — towers for midgets, shorn
Of all their promise—we still hail the morn,
Acclaim as promised lights the lamps we see.

Savour the pottage then, and earn its hire,
Freedom for soul and body, life and light . . .
Happy the very beasts of those that buy

The magic dreams? Come tread them in the mire!
O fools, we dreamt, we who would purify,
Thirsty for words of truth, limpid and bright.

122

VI

Thirsty for words of truth, limpid and bright,
We pay the traders' double tax and toll
With sap of guileless youth, unflawed and whole,
Our warmth of spring, as with its rippling might

Like pagan springs from caverns of the night . . .
Till age and weakness come, snake-like, the soul
Sloughs off its skin and shelters in a hole,
And through the lattice now there winks no light.

O dreams of youth, O fleeting butterflies!
You blossomed with the flowers — where do they bide?
And you were silent when the birds'-song died.

Where are you, hero, brave of finger height?
Stumbling you fell mid vanities and lies
From trap to pit, from shadows to the night.

VII

From trap to pit, from shadows to the night
We fall, smouldering remnant from the fire,
With a polluted blessing to inspire,
Glibly we praise our 'Reason' — the false light

That lulls our spirit to forget its plight,
With wealth of joy and music of the lyre;
With boundaries, rules and laws do we acquire
Civilized theories, crass and erudite.

Like tiny children let us be once more,
A drop amid the flood, the meadow's sighs.
No search, no goal, no rule, no tyranny.

As we were once in olden times, before
We reigned o'er earth and light, ere we grew wise
And we were tired by seers of prophecy.

VIII

And we were tired by seers of prophecy
Who longed to save the world and all mankind,
Spreading their gospel, patient and resigned,
Covering the world with altars like a sea.

Humble perforce, white lambs of sanctity
Till they inherit — Then oppress and grind,
Pillage and slay like ravening wolves entwined
With laurel wreaths and flaunting garlandry.

Could but the endless rivers of the blood
Shed by these hungry, holy hangmen flood
The Hejaz sands and stones of Galilee,

Then they would bloom for all eternity,
The wilderness become a grassy dell —
Cursed be the priests of idols and of Bel!

IX

Cursed be the priests of idols and of Bel,
The setters-up of gods and heavenly thrones,
Who write their faith on parchment and on stones
With signs and wonders, witnesses to tell.

Who offer cash for faith to those who sell;
And thunderous gods and judges with harsh tones,
And white and stupid fiery orbs and cones,
Mightily bidding joy to rise and swell.

Upon their altars too, where they revere,
They offer blood, a sacrificial toll,
Bring countless thousands to the slaughter-post,

All those that will not dance amid their host,
The generous of heart and pure of soul,
Prophets of truth, and those who give them ear.

X

Prophets of truth, and those who give them ear . . .
They bear a two-edged weapon in their hand:
Love and the Truth, a wonder-working brand;
They sow their seed with prayer far and near,

On brazen souls and stony hearts long sere,
Beguile the good, outwit the evil band,
Through blood and fire they preach in every land
With zealot folly, stubborn without fear.

But falsehood reigns, and truth is hid and spurned,
And love ferments like leaven in a bowl
And stinks on pyres where heretics are burned.

And every thinker has become a knell,
Though some were saved, he did not save their soul.
Let world-reformers rot in endless hell.

XI

Let world-reformers rot in endless Hell!
Gelded of heart and tortuous of goal,
With sightless mind and with forsaken soul,
While their Hell gapes, of Heaven's joys they tell;

Rush on their way like stupid clods, pell-mell,
Shattering and rending with unending toll
The Grecian statues and the artists' scroll,
They do not hear the soul of man rebel.

Until they rule and hide themselves on high
They prate of justice, sing of liberty,
Bold levellers who slay in sanctity;

With chains and gallows do they end their song
For those who will not bow, those who defy —
The priests of beauty and the artists' throng.

XII

The priests of beauty and the artists' throng,
Each pure of soul, with holy torch beside —
— And if a seed of beauty be espied
His are the lashes of the slanderer's thong.

A crown of briars — the guerdon of the strong —
Comes there a foe of beauty to deride?
Must Calvin have Servetus at his side?
Answer me, you who dream of tints and song!

We call for life from depths of nothingness
With myriad voices and a mystic cry,
But there is no lament for us, no sigh;

We scattered tints and colours as largesse;
But of the holy purple we are clear,
Followers of poesy who hold her dear.

XIII

Followers of poesy who hold her dear,
For you the past and future are the same,
In Nile-sprung hymns that bear Ikhnaton's name,
In psalms of David, welling with a tear,

A single cradle-song, that scatters cheer
On slave-born bondmaid and on high-born dame;
The weary toiler's heart shrinks as the flame
And tinted mysteries of the eve appear.

And your creation spreads a noble creed
With boundless hope, a heart afire and strong,
It gathers spark to spark and deed to deed,

Slowly, as gardens bloom with summer rain,
If such may be its fate, if God ordain,
They save the world with music and with song.

XIV

They save the world with music and with song,
And all is one great wondrous harmony,
But yet the beast of prey lurks and breaks free
In depths of man, and bursts the binding thong.

Stripped of the covering tatters that belong
To culture, it appears with evil glee.
Aeons of lofty, fine philosophy,
Knowledge and faith, what have you done so long?

The flooding streams of holy purple flow
On all the earth, man sinks in the pure sea . . .
Twilight of culture, and the boundaries fade.

Does darkness conquer, or the dawn's first glow?
We peer in wonder at the twilight shade,
Tired of mankind, the ages' legacy.

XV

Tired of mankind, the ages' legacy,
Our eyes are yearning for the distant light;
Ageing, we wait the great and wondrous sight,
We rove and seek for creeds of mystery.

We turn to streams, and paths of fantasy,
Thirsty for words of truth, limpid and bright,
From trap to pit, from shadows to the night,
And we were tired by seers of prophecy.

Cursed be the priests of idols and of Bel!
Prophets of truth and those who give them ear!
Let world reformers rot in endless Hell!

The priests of beauty and the artists' throng,
Followers of poesy who hold her dear—
They save the world with music and with song.

(*Tr.* L. Bernard)

FLOWERS

Flowers after reaping, flowers after harvest home
In empty fields, by crossroads. Lo, their fate
Is like the orphans', withered grass around,
Or like the poor who stand beside the gate.

They are like beggars knocking at the door
Who tell their woes to ears of unbelief;
They bow their heads, for they are orphan flowers.
The blessed rain falls, they find no relief.

There may be showers of blessing, breezes, calm,
But none for flowers whose passing naught can stem;
Beneath the frost they lie, where cart wheels roll,
Made for a world that was not made for them . . .

(*Tr.* L. V. Snowman)

MEMORIAL TO THE VICTIMS OF THE UKRAINE

There are many like him there — unsymbolled heap,
'Gainst which the ox will trip that treads the wheat,
And the farmer curse in anger as he ploughs;
His skull in a mound, or grasshoppers' retreat

Before the autumn. Only clouds will weep
Cold tears for him, the storm still him with scorn,
No prayers be said for him but these laments;
Footpaths will pass him by, but none to mourn.

The years roll on and level out this grave,
It wakens from its sleep all sown with tare;
The wind's in the whistling sheaves that o'er it wave.

But in the dust that hapless one rots there,
Knowing not why he is furrowed or a mound,
Or why he lived, or timeless bit the ground.

(*Tr.* L. V. Snowman)

EVENING IN THE VILLAGE

Noiseless and swift are the feet of those sweet, hidden evenings
    in winter,
Round which there hovers an air of soft sadness and meek
    melancholy,
When the earth's whiteness grows dark and the red of the sun
    grows intenser
Like a husband forsaking forever the bride of his wedlock
And in his coldness remembering the charm of her tender
    virginity:
Slowly his countenance changes, and her white features darken
    in anguish . . .
Bluish-grey clouds scud across the pale-gold expanse of the
    heavens,
Others are following and more till the south and the west are
    all covered.
Slowly they take on the form of the wing of a wondrous great
    monster,
Darkening the heavens and casting a black, heavy shade on the
    village.
Calm are the houses and silent, and each with its roof and its
    windows
And its veranda seems living. Behold there a meek, little
    dwelling;
Small are its windows; behind it there lies a neglected old
    garden,
Fixed to those grey, crumbling pillars that stand there to guard
    it from ruin.
Like a shrivelled and withered old woman who goes out in
    autumn,
Moist-eyed and broken, to gather a lettuce for supper.
Here is the lord of the houses, alone and apart in his glory,
Turbaned with new, shiny tiles, on protruding walls almost
    reclining,

And in his quizzing eye-windows a hidden smile dances and
    flickers,
Saying, "Here I am before you." How bold is the opposite dwell-
    ing!
Rakish and low are its eaves at the top of its walls white and
    lofty;
Impudently does it leer from its sparkling panes, tinted by sun-
    beams;
Low is its hat on its brow and its two bright impertinent
    windows.
Near-by there stands on a base of white boulders a concave-
    walled granary,
Shattered and broken-roofed by the fury of tempest and storm-
    wind.
Scattered around it lie sheaves, and it scornfully looks from
    closed windows
Just like a long-haired, young postal official, all pock-marked
    and pimpled.
Gazing upon it with clear eyes — another small dwelling,
Modest and flooded with light like a bride that is led to the altar,
Beautiful in her maturity, filled with a new love that blossoms —
And you would think that this building is served and attended
    by flunkeys,
As it looks forth, as if knowing and feeling its own great
    importance
Yet do its eyelids betray it, by daily profligacy weighted,
Nor do its dull, half-closed eyes make beholders respect it;
Sheaves, littered over its roof, top its windows like thick, bushy
    eyebrows.

                              (*Tr.* Thomas Silk)

BEHOLD, O EARTH

Behold, O Earth, how wasteful we have been.
Within your sacred lap, the secret dwelling-place, we hid our
    seed. No more
The glossy barley-spray, the heavy-kernelled wheat,
The gold-streaked grain of rye, the tasselled sheaf of corn.

Behold, O Earth, how wasteful we have been:
We have hidden the fairest of our flowers in you,
Those whom only the earliest rays of the sun have seen,
Whether retiring bud, or spray full of petalled incense.
Scarcely they knew of noon-tide, for their grief was innocence,
And before the dewdrops were dried they were caught in a
    light that was new.

Take to yourself, then, the best of our children, youth of the
    purest dream
Wholehearted, clean-handed, untouched by the world's malady.
And the web of their days still half-woven, a web of the life yet
    to be.
We have no better than these. What better than these have you
    seen?

Cover them over yourself. In its hour the corn will be green,
A hundred times stronger in glory, as the land is, in sanctity,
Splendid amends for our lives be their sacrifice, in death's
    mystery.
Behold, O Earth, how wasteful we have been.

(*Tr.* Hilda Auerbach)

Zalman Shneur (1887-1959)

THE DARK AGES DRAW NEAR
(extracts)

Again the Dark Ages draw near. Do you hear, do you feel,
    man of spirit,
The stir of the whirling dust, the distant odour of brimstone?
And oppressive foreboding hid in the air, in the heart, in the
       land,
As at times of eclipse of the sun, when houses grow pale, seem
       to quake,
And the blue of the skies turns to lead, and the cattle start
       lowing with fear,
And herbs and trees become pallid like foliage grown in cellars,
And the faces of men are rigid, grotesque as masks of wax?
It is the old, dark cloud returning from the mediaeval past,
As rivers return to the sea and the sun to the clouds of the west.
The ancient wheel rotates with its olden, rusty screech,
The tide of blood has stirred it, like a river that suddenly bursts
The desolate millwheel — abode of ravens and demons;

Not moistened enough is its axle, and it shrieks and curses from
      drought,
And the dust of its former victims rises straight from its cracked
      teeth,
The gloom of the Goths arises in fire and terror on the skyline;
Thus was it ever, and thus Fate returns once more to our people,
After each message of spring, seven thick snowstorms and
      tempests.
The conquering peoples have become heirs to the treasures of
      their land;
Day, darkness, summer and winter return again and again;
Love, hate, innocence, shrewdness . . . and thus it is for all time;
Keen is the coming winter, for summer was long on the earth, —
    The Dark Ages draw near!

    . . . has your heart heard in the night
A distant and evil noise of nails scratching in the darkness?
It is the dragon of the Dark Ages turning to slough off his skin.
In the Age of Renascence he trembled, coiled up, slept the sleep
      of death.
Too tight for him was his old skin, he slept in order to change it;
He was dumb in a seeming cramp, as a reptile basks in the sun,
Fields of produce grew in his cheeks and vines wound about his
      neck;
They chained him with tubes of iron and brass and railroad
      tracks,
And subject peoples presumed to erect their shrines on his back;
Slaves went forth to feast their triumph on his slumbering form
With banners and medley of songs, proud and haughty they
      spoke,
They said, "See, he is dead and will never revive." They knew
      not
That his sombre strength was preserved, the mockeries of the
      Dark Ages.
As one day to the basking reptile are ten jubilees of slumber,
As one day to this monster are the long annals of peoples.

But now he is ready, too long pent up in his old skin. Beware!
Soon he will burst the coat on which gardens and cities have
       sprung,
And rend the bonds of culture which will be like singed flax;
And the enraged mediaeval monster will issue from the ruins,
Huge and strong as of yore, blazing from the depths of his eyes,
His skin bristling with spears and steam hissing in his throat,
And factories belching smoke from his nostrils breathing murder,
Exhaling short blasts with the odour of burning petrol.
And where will his great egg, big as the earth, be hatched?
We know not, we cannot tell . . .
What boots it for us all, scattered about the earth, to know?
Wherever we turn the calamity will overtake us first.
    The Dark Ages draw near!

(Tr. L. V. Snowman)

UP TO PRAYER!

At midnight the village idiot crouched on the lifeless jelly
That had been the Rabbi and now lay there, with his own blood
    smeared,
And tickled his upturned heel and pulled at his mud-stained
    beard,
And with sudden vehemence leapt up and kicked his back and
    belly:

"Get up, you souse, up to prayer! In the dirty ditch
You've fallen asleep half-dressed, bare-headed, in vomit and
    grime.
O dear, what a sight! Where are your shoes, your *shtreiml?*
Look at you, rolling here in the dirt like a drunken bitch!

He-he, up to prayer! No shirking! Come, lean on my arm.
I'll drag you to synagogue whether you like it or lump it,
And seat you on a pile of human dung among the shattered
    doors.

There a dog's corpse instead of a chandelier is swinging —

And from a tattered scroll your cut throat will trumpet
Into the ears of your raped daughters, your grandson who lies
    there, charred,
And the beadle's ears, split by the hooves of the horse.

                    (*Tr.* A.B.)

SONG OF THE MAN OF SPIRIT
(extracts)

Who is as bountiful, who as miserly as I?
I search in every dunghill, in every dismal pit,
Gather all my life, and purify, and add
Spark to spark and drop to drop of beauty
For those who inherit it.
Where are the heirs and who are the heirs?
Behold, I see them,
A herd of blind and cunning sucklings
Stealing the inheritance while yet I live,
Sniffing and wrinkling their cold, black snouts,
Creasing their low beast-brows,
Evil in their bloodshot eyes and treachery in their tails;
And I look forth from my creator's window
And listen attentively
To all that those wild beasts below are whining.
And who knows their herd and their baseness as I do?
They rejoice over my fall as if they had conquered,
And the faults in my work are victories to them.
And when I rise full height in all my strength
Their praises pour forth like a flood of spittle.
When I lie down, my work done,
They lick my dripping sweat
And murmur, "We have conquered, we are weary!"

. . . .

From the four winds of heaven a silent voice calls,

In the stillness of forest and mountain I hear it, —
The Voice
"Be silent and create!
From the fragments of your life build temples for others,
Hate them all and command them to love
But ask not 'why.'

. . . .

And sometimes, when you kneel under the yoke,
When you are torn between loathing and lust for creation,
Then sing to yourself
The song of comfort for creators,
The song of the captive princess."

Woe to you, O captive princess
In the palace of the Sultan!
Downy carpets of the tyrant
Chafe your tender flesh like gravel;
And like sorcerers' eyes, his jewels
Peer and spy, seek to bewitch you
Lest you flee,
And should he approach your slumber
In the moonlight nights of sadness
With the plumes of birds of Eden
Rearing from his green-hued turban,
And his curved and glittering sabre
Like a crescent in his girdle,
Savage splendour in his features . . .
Then you know he comes to quell you;
Weep upon your scattered tresses,
Weep upon your heaving bosom,
Know that you are still a captive
And the palace walls are mighty;
By the gates are shades and Negroes
Leaning on their tapering lances —
And you bear your shame in silence

As becomes a suffering princess:
Tight-shut mouth and eyes wide open.
At the stranger's lust consuming
Drinking from your sacred fountain.
Till at last you too grow thirsty
In the silence and the darkness
And you drink the savage power
In your fever, like the waters
Of a muddled desert spring.
And perforce you too are sated
With his love.
Like a tiger and a tigress
Beasts of prey amid the shadows
Of an eastern night, and biting,
Full at once of lust and spite . . .
As the greenish sparks are shooting
From their manes and eyes,
Filtered moonlight falls upon you
Through the silken, broidered hangings,
Misty, blue, intoxicating,
Like the fumes of heavenly incense;
And you laugh when he goes from you,
Know that you will be a mother;
Loveless for your tyrant master
Twofold love you bear your children.
And when captive you are gathered
To your people, you will die
With no husband's love, but sated
With constraint and palace splendours.

(*Tr.* L. Bernard)

THIS IS NO COMMON BREEZE

This is no common breeze, this is no stormy gust,
This is no fleeting mist, this is no sweeping rain,
This is no twilight hour, this is no pallid dawn,
This day there is no joy, this day there is no pain.

Not to embrace a girl nor yet to rot alone,
You do not dream the future, nor recall things that were;
As you begin the task — so you already yawn,
As you seek idleness — so your heart yearns for care.

Sometimes you seek but this, to lie in silent sleep,
Sleep that is free from dreams, sleep that is dull and still,
Sleep till the summer wakes you with its glow,
Sleep till the storm of snow wakens you with its chill.

(*Tr.* L. Bernard)

Avraham Shlonsky (1900-   )

AT THE END OF THE NIGHTS

I

Everything goes into hiding yet dazzles.
Everything screams 'I exist not!' yet stays.
Everything falters, too baffled to frazzle
Your X-raying gaze.

Is that why we quailed, sorely tempted to run
Away from the good and to welcome the wicked?
If only we managed, O Tangible One,
To take our eyes off the trigger!

But you, too, are weary of playing acquitter
And once more ensnare us, hellbound.
And once more a steely-eyed boa-constrictor
Is holding us riveted, spellbound.

II

To you and to you, to the end of the nights,
To the margin of days, never dead though extinguished;
Where, turgid as dunes, all the crimes of mankind
Swell up unredressed, unrelinquished.

Look at a man's hand: it's crying out.
Look at his soul: it's afraid to borrow.
Condone his embarrassment, honour his doubts,
The tortuous grin that betrays his horror.

Hosanna, Hosanna, yet no succour comes!
If you have forgotten to grasp and forbear,
Then spare us your watchfulness' bonus,
Have mercy upon us
And let us repair

III

To a morn that will see our hand caressing
The grass and its dew,
The kid and its wool.
To a pair of syllables' constant blessing
Wherever our babies will stammer and pule.

To a first-born fear,
To a primal awe —
How you appeared
Like all of us: smiling, erratic and bothered.
Till you came to your senses and wilfully bowed
The shoulders of trees and the heads of mothers.

Our father, he loved the laden fertility
of trees that bent down,
Of branches that stirred.
Pray teach us to greet, to obey with humility
The grace of your patience,
The scope of your world.

* The word is used here in the ancient Hebrew sense, as an appeal for deliverance, not in the Christian laudatory sense.

IV

The gist of Creation looked perfect when hither
You brought us, O planter of planets and crescents.
How eager to ripen, how ready to wither
Are all those fine limbs that beleaguer our essence.

Stop gazing at us like a hostile surgeon,
Besprinkle in us every fibre and root.
O teach us to smile on our birth like a burgeon,
At death to be still like the garnered fruit.

(*Tr.* A.B.)

TINY FEET
(from *Song to Mummy and Daddy*)

We had tiny feet
(Mummy-Daddy's joy, God's little chicklets).
O how we loved to dip them in the puddles
And watch them wallow in the mud like piglets!

The rains are a godsend to the waiting peasant,
To the carefree fields of wheat,
But a thousand thousand times more pleasant
To those who have tiny feet.

How welcome are tiny feet on the sward
It ravaged, far-off spots,
And blessed, blessed be the Lord
Who lavishes rain on the tots.

(*Tr.* A.B.)

Avraham Shlonsky 41

TILLER OF THE GROUND

> *"But Cain was a tiller*
> *of the ground."*
> (*Gen.* 4:4)

A camel and plough. The blade and its colter
Toiling hard to dissever clod from clod.
Never were the eternities so clasped in one moment,
The world so single in plot.

Here's the hint of murder,
Here's the blade pressing forward,
Here's Cain who the unity of clod dares defy.
Never was distance so gaugeable, finite,
Between man
And camel
And sky.

(*Tr.* Dov Vardi)

WORK

The palm of our hand is small and five are its fingers,
Thin fingers of wax and all too fragile,
A pulse at their roots, their tips — nails.
What will be done to our fingers on the day we employ
   them?
Throb mightily, my pulse. Wildly grow, my nails —
We are going to work.

O fortunate fingers, holding the sickle in harvest,
Hugging the clod covered with nettles,
Tell us:
What will be done to these fingers so tender?

O sweat,
O beaded benedictions gliding from the height of my
   forehead
As dew from the lucid heavens.

Behold, my flesh is pure and hairy,
Its hair is dusky grass.
O sweat, salt sweat,
Make my flesh dewy, turgid as fields in the morning.
Praise, Halelujah.

The morning skies lift the thick boughs of an oak,
Absalom's head, golden, curly,
Hangs high in the branches above —
Sun, O Sun!

I will stoop to the sands.
Beneath the heavy concrete, dunes gasp:
O Man, why did you come to the deserts
To anchor the bit in our mouths?
A wind lashes suddenly from the east
And like herds of wild unbroken camels
Sweep down on the suburb in building —
Sands!

They gallop like hail on road and foundations;
With lilliput shoes
The granular sand-hoofs
Pellet my face.
Vengeance!
Now behold — they wheel — they shriek:
To the deserts, the deserts!

Slow my hand —
The spade in my hand is gray with cement —
The roads twist in pursuit: Follow after!
The hands stretch:
Crush them! Cramp them!
Harness the deserts,
Tighten the reins of the roads
For it is I sitting high at the wheel,
I — work.

Huge fists crouch in the sands:
Houses — houses — houses —

I sense:
It is I who is caught in the branches of dawn.
As a ray in my hand gleams a spade.
And the unfinished suburb grins at me, laughs:
Sun, O Sun!

Dress me, mother dear, in a coat of splendid colours
And lead me to work with dawn.
My country is wrapped in a *talith* of light.
The houses project like frontlets —
Like *tefillin* thongs dip the roads bedded by our hands.
The lovely suburb chants a psalm of dawn to its Maker,
And among the makers — your son, Avraham,
Poet-Roadbuilder in Israel.

Father will return from his sufferings with dusk
And murmur his pleasure in prayer:
Avraham is my one dear son,
Just skin and sinew and bone —
Praise! Halelujah!

Dress me, mother dear, with a coat of splendour,
And at dawn lead me
To work.

                              (*Tr.* Dov Vardi)

A HOTEL ROOM

The room here is right-angled, as in all hotels,
But very long
And not too high
And narrow.
Here in the gloom you manage all too well
To whisper 'God' in adolescent terror.

To press a torrid brow against a window-pane
(The eye, you know, can hear at such an hour),
And like a hound whose master has been slain,
Frustrated silence in the darkness howls.

At such an hour, by inspiration's chord,
A perfect square of loftiness is twisted,
And my attentive eyes an alien town behold
Unfolding like a train's nocturnal vista.

(*Tr.* A.B.)

ENVY

I do not envy you your stellar riches
In alienated distances,
O Turning Sword of Solitude.

I'd rather have this forest
Where treetops touch befriendingly
And trunks are worlds apart.

The wind, caressing oaks and bushes
As if they both were new-born babes,
Will now play havoc with my hair until
Some birds mistake it for a tree and seek
To build a nest there for their fledgelings.
And God, so merciful and kind,
Tired of the ruthless grandeur,
Will turn His eyes from His abysmal heavens
And see that my abode is good.

But oh, the feller, Father, oh, the headsman —
I hear his footsteps,
I see his swinging arms
And envy then the quietude of stars.

(*Tr.* A.B.)

HAIL

When treetops clatter on a stormy night
One seems to hear a distant rumbling sound:
Stars falling prostrate on the ground
As ripe fruit fall down when you shake a tree.

And then
When even roots' complacence is disturbed
They may console themselves, safe in the clods,
And say,
"How wise indeed we were to hide so deep."

But what will God's birds do
When hailstones pelt them in the open sky?

(Tr. A.B.)

Avigdor Hameiri (1887-   )

THE HUT

Fruit of the goodly tree, leaves of the palm tree,
Branch of the myrtle, and willows of the stream —
God of every fearful hour,
In this forest of horrors, guard Thou my hut,
Hut of young shoots, hut of creativity,
From the conjurings of men, and men that come of lions.

Fruit of the goodly tree, branch of the myrtle,
Willows of the stream, and leaves of the palm tree —
God of every pleasant hour,
In this forest of horrors, never fête for victory,
No exulting over spoils, and no paean after battle;
Here in the straits, guard Thou this hut of mine.

Fruit of the goodly tree, willows of the stream,
Leaves of the palm tree, and branches of myrtle —
God of each eternal hour,
In this forest of horrors, only this coign is for me,
In all of the earth, and in all of heaven.
Perhaps, perhaps, perhaps, Thou'll not move me again?

(*Tr.* Jacob Sloan)

ORPHANS

He who never tasted
The sweet kisses of Mum
Will remain dumb.

In vain he shouts,
Working his hands like pistons —
No one listens.

He who was never sated
By the bliss that mothers yield
Will remain unfilled.

In vain he stays
Guzzled and drunk —
His palate is shrunk.

One to whose rescue
No guiding hand came
Will remain lame.

In vain he scales mountains:
He always rolls back
Into a chasm, pitch-black.

And none send after him
On the brink of Hell
A whisper of 'Farewell.'

(*Tr.* A.B.)

Isaac Lamdan (1899-1954)

MASSADAH*
(excerpts)

I. *I Was Told*

One autumn night, on a makeshift couch, far from our ravaged home, my mother died.

A last tear froze in her eyes as she whispered me a dying blessing, before I went away to foreign fields with a kitbag heavy on my shoulder.

On Ukrainian paths, dotted with graves and swollen with pain,
My brother fell dead and was buried in a heathen grave.
Only Father clung to the doorpost grovelling in the ashes
And murmured a prayer over the profaned name of God.
While I, girding my soul with the last iron girders of courage,
Fled at midnight to the exile ship bound for Massadah.

I was told

There the banner of rebellion has been unfurled,
  demanding retribution from Heaven and Earth, God and
  Man.

* See Glossary and Notes. 'Massadah' is used here symbolically.

Against the fate of generations a breast is bared with a roar:
  "Enough! You or I! Here the battle will decide
    The final verdict!"

I was told

  Among the walls of Massadah prophets wander, prophesying
    redemption,
  And in the tabernacles, among the ramparts, the Levites are
    singing 'To The Victor'
  And tomorrow's echo answers 'Amen Selah.'
  There the young priests stretch out the arms of mercy to
    the orphaned sky
  And pray for the full moon to be restored.

I was told

  On the warriors' heads
  Has descended the Divine Presence,
  Brimming with atonements,
  And through the curtain of things to come
  The great eye of Dawn
  Is watching over Massadah.

II. *The God of Vengeance*

A friend met me in my flight and called to me in the darkness:
A myth, this Massadah of yours, a new trap laid by Fate in
  mockery of the last survivors.
The curse has been poured into our blood, it is oil to the wick
  of our life. The wick will not burn without it,
    even in Massadah.
Where will you flee now that the shadow of dread is bound
  unto you as the head is bound unto the shoulders?
How can you leave behind you the tight fists of graves,
  congealed in their fury against the outthrust tongue,
    whirling about between the furthermost horizons?

Who will avenge the blood of brothers and sisters, of fathers
and sons, drunk in like wine by the earth — and she,
the whore, has not spewed it out?
"There is no way, none!" roars even mute and empty space.
Continents, seas and heavens have conspired against the
few of us, and all the gods and devils have joined in the
conspiracy and signed it with our blood.
Come, my friend, let us serve the One who will gather us in.
A heavy night has descended on the world — come, let us
strangle the sun of tomorrow while it is yet in the
swaddling-clothes of its twilight, that it be not appeased
with fresh mornings.
The world has gone off orbit. Let us pour confusion into its
blood till it reels and staggers like a drunkard and never
finds its path again.
Let us tangle the net of its paths until, lost and exhausted,
it falls wounded and weary and aches like us, like us!
Here is spread out a red cloak — a new striped coat that
the priests and prophets of the world have fashioned for
the festival of its happiness, for tomorrow.
The cloak is long and broad — come, let us wrap ourselves
and all the world in it.
Let us wrap up the world and embrace it with love, with love,
and as we embrace it we shall thrust a knife into its belly,
swollen with overindulgence in our own flesh, that
the embryo of its happiness may drown in its blood
whilst still in the womb of space.
The God of Vengeance — One is He Who covers us with
His wings when our tired heads are bared of all protection.
Come, let us set up an altar for Him, be His priests in the
Temple.
This is the duty of every young man among the last survivors
of Judaea.
So raise not your eyes to the lie that shines bright from afar
and misleads. Do not go. Massadah is a myth, a delusion.

(*Tr.* Leon Yudkin)

JONAH FLEES FROM HIS GOD

> *"And Jonah arose to flee to*
> *Tarshish from before the Lord. . . .*
> *And the Lord cast a great wind into*
> *the sea, and there was a great storm."*
> *(Jonah* 1:3-4)

You have found me, O my God. Between the sea and the sky
has Your tempest caught up with me.

Alas, I did not ask: "Can a man flee from his shadow, or can a
tree

Tell its roots, Let go of me, my children of darkness

That I, the trunk, may· wander off alone?

Now I know: there is but one way by which a man is brought
to his fate,

And there are seventy-seven by which he may flee but not
escape.

I thought, A man may lie down and sleep at the bottom of a
boat,

And not be the son of Amitai who is too weary to sustain his
truth,

Not Jonah whose burthen burns within him like a fiery coal,

Whose vision creeps on him like a hissing army of serpents, —

But simply a man with no yoke, with no double life,

A bundle of dust and ashes, living serenely on a cradle of
waves,

A man without care, looking at people and nations

As one looks at the stars whose course never changes.

But now Your tempest has caught me, and I know not which
is angrier

— My heart, held in Your palm, or this sea raging in its fury

To assault the boat for having offered refuge to a man who,
from the womb, was destined to be denied refuge?

O my God, My Persecutor, why do you place such a burden
on me?

Tell me, what have I taken with me that the world will miss when I have fled?

Why do you hound me so? Is the key to the Universe concealed on my person?

Will the sun not rise and set when I am gone?

Will the world's sounds be silenced when I am silent?

Will the earth become barren and the trees withold their fruit if I do not carry my burden?

No, I shall return no more. I swear it. I shall speak no more.

I shall flee, though I know that my pursuer and persecutor is within me.

I shall go far from land and never consent to mediate
Between God and Man, Earth and Heaven
And be a constant target for the arrows of both.

No more will I be catapulted in The Great Sling,

No more will I consent to receive either the corn of the land or the choice fruits of Heaven.

No more will I be a stray waif on Your earth.

If You despise me when I transgress against Your wishes —

Who am I that there should be a storm because of me? How much of a thorn in Your side can I be?

Why should You stir the depth of the sea and the host of its waves just because of me?

And if I am so dear to You, why don't you let me go in peace?

I swear I shall never return. Is there nowhere among the crannies of the world

A retreat, a refuge for me as there are cities of refuge for murderers?

Why should You withhold sanctuary from a man who has murdered his peace of mind

And thrown the pieces to others who did not want them?

Is there not a corner where, like the tree of the field, I could stand silent and suck in Your light from above and the darkness of Your earth from below,

Where I could bend my head with the changing seasons, before the press of Your storms?

Is there not among the stones of Your fields a headstone
On which I could rest my head at eventide to the echo of
parting day,
That I might sleep without the terrors of dreams? Without
the dread of visions?
Let me flee there, to a landscape where I know nothing
Except the kindness of the transient, and the pick of the
grape harvest of every passing year.
Oh, let me be! Every rising wave, like a titanic arm,
Exalts itself against me to gather me and turn me back.
But I have decided to return no more.
Arise, O storm, cast me to the depths like a discarded stone,
destroy me as a mariner is destroyed.
Let the waves drown me, let the great deep swallow me,
That there should no longer be a Jonah Ben Amitai in the
land,
Servant of God and His truth, bound to the train of His
splendour,
Who is dragged in the dust of the earth.

                                        (*Tr.* Leon Yudkin)

THE GREEN DREAM

Bereaved and despoiled we went forth from the great storm of
        the world
And dark confusion lowered from the slits of our lightless eyes.
Lost is our precious talisman from the pierced scrip of our
        wandering
In strange, rich fields of affliction we went forth to glean after
        the reapers.

Wretched and poor indeed.
All our companion lights have grown dim, towards the one light
        still we go:
The light of the green dream, that appeared like a mother's ghost
To comfort her straying, orphan son —

Tidings of fields, bringing peace and redemption, caress our
  withered sterility.

In our heavy ears the rustle of corn and trees whispers new love
And our dry nostrils expand to the scent of earth and rain.
To the last green dream our arms are stretched out, beseeching,
And the dry stalks of our fingers yearn towards it with a last
  longing —
To bloom!
And great is the fear for the interpretation, and terror walks in
  our depths,
O Lord God of the wanderers, will they bloom? —
For whither then shall we turn our shattered body, bare of
  verdure or flower,
And what path is there in our barren land if the green dream
  too is false?

(*Tr.* L. Bernard)

Avraham Ben-Itzhak (1883-1950)

BLESSING

Blessed are those who sow and do not reap
Because they wander far.

Blessed are those who give themselves freely, the splendour
Of whose youth has added to daylight
Though they flung off their glory where roads part.

Blessed are those whose pride crosses the borders of their souls
And becomes a white humility
After the rainbow's rising in the cloud.

Blessed are those who know what their heart cries out in desert
And on their lips silence flowers.

Blessed are they, for they will be taken into the heart of the
    world
Wrapped in a cloak of unremembrance,
Speechless for ever.

(Tr. Arthur Jacobs)

AVENUE IN ELLUL*

Lights that are dreaming,
Lights whitening,
At my feet are falling,
Shadows that are soft,
Tired shadows,
Fondle my path.

Between bared tree heights
A little wind
Moves sound
And hushes.
A last leaf
Floats downwards,
Trembles for one moment —
Then turns to silence.

(*Tr.* Arthur Jacobs)

* Ellul — the last month in the Jewish calendar year, corresponding roughly to August-September.

Leah Goldberg (1911-   )

THE LOVE OF THERESE DU MEUN

Note by Leah Goldberg. Thérèse du Meun was a woman of the French aristocracy who lived at the end of the sixteenth century in the environs of Avignon, in Provence. When she was about forty years old, she fell in love with a young Italian who was tutoring her sons, and dedicated to him forty-one sonnets. When the young Italian left her house, she burned all her poems and sought the seclusion of a nunnery. The memory of her poems remained only as a legend transmitted by her contemporaries.

(The following two sonnets are taken from the twelve which Leah Goldberg has 'reconstructed,' as it were, from the above-mentioned poems, irretrievably lost.)

Sonnet III

If you discarded me, expelled me far
Into the wilderness, a prey to sorrow,
To death, starvation, loneliness and horror,
As Abraham drove his concubine, Hagár —

157

If callously you let my heartblood drip,
If like a slut you had me grieved, insulted,
Not thus would my hurt feelings have revolted,
Nor my defiance be so bitter, crisp.

But you regard me as a highborn dame,
An inaccessible, exalted lady,
You hardly even dare pronounce my name.

A lofty castle, fortified and blocked.
With fear of shame my steps are stilted, shady,
My fists are hammering against the rock.

Sonnet VIII

The raindrop filaments, like strings, close tight
Upon the window-pane. My friend, please kindle
The hearth-fire. Let us sit among the lights
And watch the silhouettes between us dwindle.

How well you fit into the greyish guise
Of rainy days. Your youthfulness is caught then
Against a double light of flame and autumn —
My heart the ardour and my mind the ice.

How much I relish this delicious fraud:
To hide my passion in maternal rolls
Of prudent care, yet leave the spell unbroken.

Nor will your brow be clouded by the thought
That here, right here before the glowing coals,
An hour of love I pilfered as a token.

(*Tr.* A.B.)

SONGS OF THE FOXES

> *"Catch us the foxes, the little*
> *foxes, that gnaw at our vines*
> *when the vines are in bloom."*
> (*Song of Solomon* 2:15)

I

Two things: the autumn and the fox in the secret places of the wood still speak to me from my pretty, fairy-taled childhood in a riddle-enchanted language as clever and chiaroscuro as a smile covering sadness.

Both are elusive gold. "I'm yours, yours," says a fall leaf gliding with the twilight breeze. "I'm yours, yours," so through the ferns, the golden red-skin, the wise-eyed creature beckons me.

My heart dashes in their footsteps, my simple heart, through tangled paths until suddenly, I understand, in them there is the eternity of separation: life on the border of its death. Stand still, my heart, until the day you tire of the chase.

When my autumn comes, I'll tread the gold of leaves and, in the ephemeral splendour, I shall see how across the way the eyes of foxes light up for me, full of the cunning of death.

II

The spoilers of the vineyards, the little foxes
In the vineyards are the footprints of foxes
How beautiful is my vineyard with its ripe grapes.

How can we hunt you, little foxes, how can we catch
you, we do not know. Can one hunt in garden paths
and lock a legend in a cage?

Who can catch golden smiles, who can hunt elusive love?
Tomorrow I shall bless the footprints in the sand
and my looted vineyard.

(Paraphrased by Ezra Spicehandler)

IN THE HILLS OF JERUSALEM

I

As stone among these ridges, I lie
In the sere, sallow grass burnt by summer,
Mute and indifferent.
Pale skies reach down to the rock.
How came a yellow-winged butterfly to this place?
A stone among stones — I do not know
How ancient my life is
Nor who may yet come along
And dislodge me with his leg
So that I go rolling down.

Perhaps this is the beauty forever cold.
The eternity
Perhaps,
Stalking slow and old.
Or maybe
The dream of death
And the single love.

As stone among these slopes I lie
In thorn and thistle,
Across the road gliding toward town.
Come, wind that blesses all,
And stroke the tops of pine
And silent stone.

II

All those things
Which are beyond love
Occur to me now —
This landscape and the wisdom of age
It has, wanting to survive
One more generation, two, three,
One eternity more.

To grow thorns without end,
To rock dead stones to sleep
Like babes in their cradle.
To be silent with old memories,
One more, two, three . . .

O, how great's the will to live
Of those about to die.
How terrible the desire
And how hollow —
To be, to be
Another year, another year,
One more generation, two, three,
One eternity more.

III

How did such a cheerful bird stray
Into these hills?
A love-call in its throat,
Its small heart trembling with love's delight —
O, it will have fledgelings in its nest,
The flight of its wings is a song of love.

And suddenly
From the heights of the blue
There appeared below it
A wasteland pelted with stone.

Rescue it,

Rescue it,
That its eyes may not see
The corpses of all loves,
The graves of all delight.

In the blue
Altitudes,

Suspended
With desolate love song,
It cannot comprehend
This death
Down below.

IV

How can a single bird
Bear all the heavens
On soft
Wings
Above the waste?
So huge and blue,
Resting on its wings,
They sustained by the power of its song.

So my heart bore its love,
It was vast and blue
And high above the altitudes,
Above the waste,
Above the heaps of ruin
And the gulfs of grief.

Until the song of my heart was silenced,
And its strength failing,
It became stone
And dropped.

My speechless, wounded love,
How can a single bird
Bear all of heaven!

(*Tr.* Dov Vardi)

EARLY SPRING

Humming stillness. April's close.
A pail the well arouses.
On the doorstep in repose
The beggar-woman drowses.

Sallow, dry and dessicate
As mushrooms from the forest,
Slow her bonnet undulates
Above her modest forehead.

And those wrinkles which corrode,
Which ramify her visage, —
Each a way, and each a road
Marked by her life's long passage.

On her bosom, a bright mole,
Snug like a cat and carefree.
Wind awakes a bell to toll
Faint from a distant belfry.

Now quickened is the day to song,
Through her its tremor races:
In her dreams she jogs along
The cool, wide-open spaces.

(*Tr.* Dov Vardi)

SONGS OF THE RIVER

"A choir of little voices."
Paul   Verlaine

I.   *The River Sings to the Stone*
I kissed the stone in her dream's cold domain,
For she is the silence and I the refrain;
For I am the seeker and she is the sought —
From one eternity we two were wrought.

The lonely cold flesh of the stone I kissed.
She's the vow to be true, I — the one who betrays,
For I am the passing and she — what exists,
She's Creation's deep secrets, and I — their display.

And I knew I had touched on a heart mute and furled,
I am a poet and she is the world.

II. *The Tree Sings to the River*

River that bore away the gold of my autumn,
That drew off my blood among fallen leaves,
That will not see the day when my spring must return
To him, with the time of the year.

My brother the river, forever the lost one,
Now every day different and the same thing —
My brother the current between his two banks
Flowing like me between autumn and spring.

For I am the bud and I am the fruit,
I am my future and past all along,
I am the trunk standing lonely, apart,
And you — you're my time and my song.

III. *The Moon Sings to the River*

I am the single one on high,
I am the many in the depths.
Look up from the river at me,
My image, my double face.

I am the truth up on high,
I am the myth in the depths.
Look up from the river at me,
My image, false in its fate.

On high I'm enveloped in silence,
I resound and sing in the depths.
Up above in the skies I am God,
In the river I'm prayer and praise.

IV.   *The Girl Sings to the River*

Where is the current taking my little face?
Why is he tearing my eyes?
My home is far off in a forest of pines,
The bark of my pines sadly cries.

The river tempted me with his joyous song,
Calling my name like a brother.
I went to him when I heard the sound,
And left the house of my mother.

And I am her only one, so young in years,
And before me a cruel river lies —
Where is he taking my little face?
Why is he tearing my eyes?

V.   *The Blade of Grass Sings to the River*

For little ones like me too,
One of a multitude,
For the children of the poor
On a shore that's destitute,
The river hums and murmurs
With love and plenitude.

The sun with warm caresses
Will touch him all around,
And my form too impresses,
Reflects in the water's bounds.
And in the depths of the river
All of us are profound.

My form, becoming deeper
On the way to the sea, its home,
Is swallowed and submerged
On the verge of the unknown —
And with the voice of the river
The soul that its silence owns,

166

To the tune of the song of the river
Will the praise of the world intone.

(Tr. Richard Flint)

WILL DAYS INDEED COME

Will days indeed come with their gift of forgiveness and blessing
And then, with a light heart and mind as a wayfarer goes,
You'll walk in the field, with the clover-leaves gently caressing
Your bare feet and stubble deliciously stinging your toes?

Or rain overtake you, its throng of drops beating aloud
On your bare, fragrant head, on your neck, on your shoulders
    and chest,
And will there expand in you, as in the skirts of a cloud,
A sunlight of quiet and rest?

And breathing the smell of the furrow that lies over yonder
You'll see the sun's rays in the puddle, a mirror of gold.
And things are so simple, alive, and a pleasure to fondle,
To love and to hold.

Alone you will walk there, unscorched by the fires, nor stumble
On highways that bristle with horror and blood; and again
In pureness' embrace you shall be meek and humble
As a blade of grass, as mere man.

(Tr. A.B.)*

* This translation benefited from a previous one (unrhymed) made by Professor S. Halkin.

Yehudah Karni (1884-1948)

EVENING IN JERUSALEM

The evening here does not approach in stealth,
  With feline bounds;
Night is no velvet of luxurious wealth
  To wrap you round.

The evening never oozes from the soul
  Until the last small drop is gone,
Nor does Night's curtain slowly fall
  Between the bright and dun.

The evening seizes, fetters,
  Hands on to the night;
The latter clutches, batters,
  Kills and buries tight.

(Tr. A.B.)

YOUR BLISS AND CALM

Pour out in me, Jerusalem, your bliss and calm.
Beneath yon skies I roam,
Where days strew rays across their palm
And stars enhance their jet nocturnal dome.

Or pin me to your folk, the chosen stem,
And I shall blindly trail behind their orbit.
Behold, your sapphired crown has caught my gem —
Your ever-studded splendour will absorb it.

Or bid me do your wish wherever needed,
Observe your pure demands in gate and cave.
Yea, though by prouder priests I am preceded
I shall but serve you better as your slave.

(*Tr.* A.B.)

Shin Shalom (1905-   )

THE DANCE OF THE TORCHES

> *"They say that on every Simkhat Beth*
> *Ha'shoëvá [Libation Festival], Rabbán*
> *Shimon Ben Gamliël used to juggle*
> *eight lighted torches in the air, throw-*
> *ing one torch and catching another, and*
> *they never touched."*
>
> (*Sukkah,*   53)

Forward, honest torch; backward, fulsome torch;
    onward, sober torch; glory is a torch.
Justice is a torch; kindness is a torch;
    nothingness a torch; everything a torch.
Throw the shackled one; catch the tackled one;
    summon glow and fun to the blazing pyre;
Crookedness is fair; circle is a square;
    sacrilege a snare; boulders — seas of fire.
Volatile and deep; diving bold and steep;
    lucid and opaque; manacled and free.

Sluggish and alert; dashing and inert;
   with discretion girt to control the spree.

  Up goes the glance,
  Down goes the dance.
  Thrill with mildness blended,
  Swing by sloth amended.
  If one torch should drop
  The whole dance will flop.

Hearts with pride will swell; hosts of Israel;
   flocks of Miriam's Well, with my heartblood watered.
Stigma, stain and stitch; arrows' flight and swish;
   tone and sound and pitch all around me quartered.
Loads of water tote for the lambs and goats;
   soon my burning throat rabid flames will swallow.
Clapping hand to hand; wielding magic wands;
   tears in silent lands with a star to follow.
Worlds to pieces fall; light disperses all;
   sparks demurely call at eternal gates.
Countless battles won; countless flickers gone;
   only Love is one, but the torches — eight!

(Tr. A.B.)

MAN AND WIFE

I wed you not with overwhelming lyre,
You won me by assurance deep and calm.
Our love-song was enhanced by wisdom's psalm,
You gave me all the light and hid the fire.

My soul was snugly sheltered in your palm
From straying wild, from deviation's briar;
And when despair would tempt me to retire,
Your tact and taste endowed me with their balm.

How good to lean my head against your breast,
The warp of sorrow and the woof of joy
To weave around your heart in peace and rest.

With me you are — who will my lot destroy?
With you I am — sleep on, 'beloved name.
I guard your altar, keep the sacred flame.

(*Tr.* A.B.)

MICHELANGELO TO THE FINGER OF GOD

Open a cleft in the marble block
To channel my blood's lively course.
Give me strength from the heart of the rock
To quarry my own resource.
Grant me a desperate need
To fashion, to knead.

Help me to flutter and hover
Along with my heaviest kit.
Give me the presence of mind to recover
My foundering wits.
Endow me with tone and nuance
That save from mischance.

Chastise me to hunger, to thirst,
From dungeons to crave for the light,
To strive though my lot be reversed
In the valley of fright,
To carve on ephemeral bark
Love's eternal mark.

(*Tr.* A.B.)

THE CAT

In my dream I dropped a ponderous weight
On the paw of a cat.
It yelled from the smart,
It clawed my lost heart.
In my dream I dropped a ponderous weight
On the paw of a cat.

In a dream none can tell
A man from a cat,
A heart from a weight.
Thus I was:
The weight that fell,
The paw,
The pain,
The pounce into space,
The terrified yell.
In a dream none can tell
A weight from a heart,
A cat from a man.

(*Tr.* A.B.)

Nathan Alterman (1910-   )

A WINTER EVENING

A storm-minded evening in winter
Its girdle of lightning boasts.
The fire-pans' red-hot cinders
Flare up in the chestnuts roast.

With hammer and saw and whittle
A carpenter plies his trade.
Perpetual screeches like fiddles,
A squeak with a zany shade.

Commences the drumming and swirling
Of copper and earthenware jars.
The trees, sorely flayed by the whirlwind,
Bend down and display their scars.

Thus flows in a workaday Orient
The music of saws and drills.
Unsung by a poet laureate
It warbles its own little trills.

A stove in an alcove's belly,
A shuffle of feet around.
The glum, wicked-looking alley
Illumines a lowering cloud.

How broad are the streets, how pretty
On wintry nights. Right away
A storm will engulf the city
And treetops will groan and sway.

A girl's hand, coy but urgent,
To fasten her dress will dart;
A hundred distracted merchants
Will trammel the flight-happy mart.

And darkness reflects in its tremor
The fire-pans' sizzles and flicks.
But what can surpass in glamour
A barbershop lit after six!

(*Tr.* A.B.)

THE PURCHASE OF THE FAIR

I

Upon the threshold of the town a fair was pitched
And there we slept beside the carts and cattle.
Till dawn, till our surroundings trembled·and unhitched
Terrific roars of throats engaged in battle.

Into the air we jumped — a chaos of affairs!
The eye beheld a multitude of goods
Unmasked in every corner. Greedy hands disperse
And fingers flutter through the cloth and foods.

Among the jostling elbows and the jogging steers
The golden money gallivants, light-footed;
And when the mule all of a sudden jibs and rears,
His sale into a circus is transmuted.

A thousand photo-snatchers and a thousand barbers,
A myriad traders, loiterers and pests,
All counted neat, except the countless thieves it harbours —
O God Almighty, what unwelcome guests!

How fortunate that I am not impressed by witches
Nor toy with fairy castles in the air;
But now, if Heaven choose to pamper me with riches,
I shall at once proceed to buy the fair.

Then at the pair of kiddies close upon my tracks
I bellowed, "Hey, why do you stand and stare?
Come, children, bring the gold and empty all the sacks
And, starting with the apples, buy the fair!"

II

Fruit-vendors heard my words and fainted. Wheel and rivet
Stood motionless and noiseless in their track.
The startled colours jumped and merged around their pivot:
Blue into white and yellow into black.

But on the vacant road we saw a man run madly
And fall and rise (for jealousy sustains):
The wild-haired moneychanger, frightened like a pedlar
Lest all the fair be purchased by the swains.

He rushed to get past me and buy from floor to pillar,
From canvas to festoon, from lollipops to snails.
O my adversary in trade, in peccadilloes,
In love and song, in toil and public sales!

And then, at my command, two heaps of goods were builded,
Upon their summits both of us stood fast,
And gambit-oaths at my opponent's head I wielded
Like flares of lightning launched before the blast.

Long live the art of swearing, bold of nerve and tendon,
Long may its beauties thunder down their mood.

Our speech disrobes in them with sudden, stark abandon
And harems rise, word-harems of the nude.

No platitudes the master of invective burgeons,
No ready-made rejoinders mar his job.
Like sea-shells he selects them, delicate and virgin,
From regions unmolested by the mob.

But imperturbably the man replied, "This jackal
And his two puppies, will they spoil our leisure?
Come, pack the fair for me — I pay two thousand *shekel* —
And stuff this trio in for goodly measure."

Two thousand? Ho-ho-ho! We laughed and cried and rumbled:
Three, seven, nine. A myriad, double, triple.
Upon our lofty heaps the golden downpour tumbled —
My riches thrashed my rival like a swipple.

Another myriad I declare. He stands aloof
And adds a thousand just to tip the scale.
And thus we strive, accompanied by throat and hoof,
To cap the climax in this gala sale.

And when the man grew pale and faltered, overpowered,
The crowd burst forward with a loud report:
"Hail, unknown knight who far above his rival towered
And bought a whole fair for the sake of sport!"

III
Said I, "O Fair, may I be changed into a barrow*
If you can find a farthing in my hems.
A pauper am I, naked as a flightless arrow,
Whose mouth is but a fountainhead of gems.

"But as the hay-carts wobble we shall rock with laughter —
So many generations, young and old —
If I, the wee one, drag you forth and ever after
Redeem you from the moneychangers' mould.

* A castrated male swine.

"Some more light-headedness, some less servility —
Just name your wish and presto! — part and parcel
Of God's own living truth — no mere similitude —
We foster from these mercenary farces.

And lest we miss our joke on such a day convivial,
Why not uproot those orders we contest,
Those calculations of profound oblivion,
And make of *them* an everlasting jest?"

But no! The market bursts with flying slate and gravel.
From roofs and eaves torrential fury flows.
A hundred fists descending hard like Doomsday's gavel —
O God Almighty, what a rain of blows!

And on that bitter day the sky and earth were jolted,
As was the poor canary in its cage,
To see how pridelessly our battered hero bolted
And ran for dear life from the market's rage.

A tender hand applies his flannel for a dressing
And both his kiddies limp upon their thigh.
The way is long. Sing, little bird, and shower blessings
On tales you shall continue by-and-by.

(*Tr.* A.B.)

THE FATHER
(from *The Song of Ten Brethren*)

Recalling the stillness of rooms and the oldness of covers
I speak — as I speak till my own daughter's eyelashes drowse —
About the good eyes, the unusual sorrow that hovers
Round Father, the head of the house.

His taut, changeless cosmos — How ample his worries, how
    wonted.

The plaint of the children his watchfulness nightly enlaces.
Alone he remains by them, stooping, unhurried, to ponder
A gloom full of flickers and shuffles and deep contemplations.

His leonine shade scales the wall, shade of illness and dungeon,
But calm is the father, no spring in his step, no rebound.
All emblems of sadness are vague, flying off at a tangent—
The sorrow that nears him is thorough, meticulous, bound.

Adroitly it strikes at his innards, a touch of the master,
A hundred and one apprehensions and Death at the threshold.
The piecemeal collapse of his body, the crack of its plaster —
He tenses and marvels, his childlike curiosity freshened.

He rises, his smile with a look of sagacity burdened.
There, there, take it quiet. Alert as a nurse, arms akimbo,
To the manacled shrieker he promises death as a guerdon,
And down goes the heart, and the senses are lucid and limber.

— He marked as a timepiece the era's events and opinions,
And when, in a farthermost alley, her senses would lighten,
Again she beheld him, the humblest of all her companions,
Who follows the moon's lonely course till the firmament whiten.

From Genesis days to this night you're a shepherd, an Abel
Woolgathering thrift, like those times when your planets you
    counted.
How deep is your mark on this earth — no desultory label —
Like veins of a leaf in the coal, pebbles grooved by a fountain.

They cherish your habit to rescue the ewe-lambs who falter —
Primeval as labour and song is a father's concern.
Your countenance pored on the brook and for ever the water
Will store it, and lick hands and ankles to greet your return.

The world is your own, is your mansion, the child that you foster,
Whose illness you carry, whose morrow you shoulder at twilight.
Its evils you face, through its dragons you walk unaccosted,
But scamper in fright from the ranters of rhetoric's highlight.

Not yours is the heretic's licence, the spite and derision
That beckon to overripe women and green poetasters.
Not yours is the glee of extremes — *you* were born to envisage
The treadmill of people, the highway routine and disasters.

Our song, has it gone to your heart? Has it reached to the
    chamber
Where shadows are walking on crutches and candle-flames
    browse? —
The lone, wakeful room where unusual sorrows encumber
The head of the house?

He marshals his powers and prudence. Abreast of him gather
His duties, ignoring the breakdown of monarchs, of princes.
Remember, our sister, the face of your friend and father
Whose heart, fond and harassed, not half of his feeling evinces.

A city besieged. Autumn thunders. The cock's ancient clarion.
Departure at hand — who will show you the soul of the world?
In minutes and seconds it lies, not in ages invariant —
How rich, how sublimely unfathomed, a moment is pearled.

Effaced is this near-timeless ant, this trackless warrior
Who trudges through annals of heartache and malice that fester.
Wicks' crackle. Fall's thunderbolts. Sharpshooting anguish.
    Memorial
Of glow and disease, cogitation till morning unrested.

A crumb of the Universe burgeons and grows from this kernel.
Here silence prevails. Iron moments. They sunder his prison.
He stoops on the cradle and rises. Yea, strength is eternal.
He whispers then, "God Save the Soul." And again, "God Save
    Reason."

(Tr. A.B.*)*

AN ANCIENT MELODY

If your tears flow at night like a river,
My joys I shall kindle like straw.
If the cold make your bones quake and shiver
I shall cover you, sleep on the floor.

Should you long for a dance, quick and pleasant,
On my very last string I shall play for you.
Should you wish for a birthday present
My life and my death I shall lay for you.

And if bread you desire or wine
I shall bow my shoulders and head,
Go out, sell these two eyes of mine,
And bring you the wine and the bread.

But if ever, while elsewhere I roam,
With your cronies you laugh and carouse,
My jealousy, tight-lipped, will come
And burn you to ash in your house.

(*Tr.* A.B.)

IN BIVOUAC

Said the bivvy, "I offer a resting-place
In my draughty and short attire,
With a warlike firmament pitching its base
On the valley of mud and mire;
With a soldier asleep — feet in outer space —
Like a tramp by the roadside fire.
And when fanes are erected with Grecian grace
And spans to the glory of Rome aspire,
No bridge nor temple will know my face,
  But I am their little sire."

(*Tr.* A.B.)

THE BOOKS
(from *The Song of Ten Brethren*)

The autumn has a tint of brass. The rising wave — an icy column.
The books, those books I can't forget,
An incandescent light.
Don't I remember how the lamplight shone upon thick volumes
And how I tiptoed after exploits late into the night.

At dead of night they came alive, and as the curtain lifted
On visions and vicissitudes and broad, fictitious streets —
Unwittingly, my friends, across the no-man's-land I drifted
And found myself encompassed by their life and feats.

When in the living land a stormy-crested cock is crowing,
His voice into the never-never-land of books will spread:
There turbulence is crystallized, precision fraught with ruin,
There silences are hanging by a thread.

But let the sign be given, let the sword be brandished
And all the hounds
Will suddenly break loose,
And lamps will flare and voices roar
And snows and summers, tightly blended,
Will battle nail-and-tooth.

And thus the books, resuscitated, throb again upon our table
And live as they have lived and strive as they have striven.
They skip no page, no jot. Would that we too were able
To pledge our hearts like them, be jealous, be forgiven!

O how I loved to startle them, to get around them, watch them
      whirling,
To chase their naked thought
Upon the circle of the lawn.
Behold her, here she comes, the Fair One, graceful like a wood-
      land yearling,
As timorous and tense as when the world was born.

Tall grows the corn, strong blows the wind upon the mountains,
Bright shines the dew on meads
Along the brooks.
Their spaciousness and grandeur are the fruit of Heaven's bounty
But their soul, brethren mine, is taken from the books.

May God preserve the scrolls for evergreen existence,
Secure from moth and mustiness and from barbarians' ire.
May angels fondly guard them from the fool's persistence
And from the bookworm's wisdom as from fire.

Well, I have spoken. But perhaps it would be better
To seal their alien love with my reluctant hand.
However, what is said can't be unsaid. My song is fettered
Unto your songs. Together they will go into the silent land.

(*Tr.* A.B.)

Itshak Tavori (1911-1944)

THIS BOY

This boy — have you oft met his like?
No gusto, no comeliness, haggard and lean.
But his gaze had the sky to imbibe and its garden to hike,
And the dew from the herbage of Heaven to glean.

This boy with his wound of a mouth tight and curled —
Every soft-moulded word was at once furnaced hard.
At the cliff of your harshness a vessel of daydreams he hurled,
And his soul and his poetry broke, shard on shard.

Strangely he flitted among you and hampered your stillness,
Upheaving the billows congealed in your hearts.
He came and he went — an oblique, flimsy illness
That soon to the depths of oblivion departs.

Have you ever divined why he came, what he wanted?
What obdurate purpose his yearnings had followed?
Like a brook of salvation he gulped your complacent decanter,
But venomous loam were the dregs that he swallowed.

He tussled with pain as he strove to resemble your image
And morselled the bread of affliction with others.
His mind was devoured by *khamsin*, fever joined in the
    scrimmage
And whispered, "Behold, I'm the comfort that smothers . . ."

Your day, ever crushed by monotony's load,
Tried to cheer and befriend this recluse, but in vain.
For grief's shadow lurked on his desolate road
And he twisted delight and he shunned merry lanes.

He passed among you as the pale moon dives
Amid sentinel beeches in grim, pensive trend.
He mustered all anguish as honey from hives
And it swarmed in voluptuous melodies, reaching no end.

The song of this boy — will you hear such again?
By greyish decree it was poured in a stuttering blend;
But sadly it clambers to loftiest, dizziest pain
That hails no beginning and hallows no end.

                                       (*Tr.* A.B.)

BEGINNINGS

Remember the days of a drunken prime
That won't be forgotten for long,
When Night knelt in tents for a rhyme
And gave us a song?

When poverty creaked in crevice and beam
But sprinkled our threshold with joyous pink,
And the moon sowed a silvery dream
On the roofs of zinc?

And now — tall houses with countenance sore
In pomp and aridity wade,
But the shy little man and his innocent lore
Are roaming, bereaved, in their shade.

And the sober day babbles and fumes,
The evening sobs under lock,
And Night is hoarse on the concrete rooms.
And Night is numb as a rock.

(*Tr.* A.B.)

Ka-Tzetnik 135633

THE CLOCK OVERHEAD
(four excerpts)

Face to Face

Naked march into the night.

Midnight silence of Auschwitz.

You cannot hear a single step from all the bare feet marching on the ground.

You do not know the length of the column in which you march, where it begins, where it ends.

Around you breathe naked human bodies, marching six abreast. Six abreast.

A transport is being led to the Auschwitz 'Bath House.'

Over your head vaults a star-sprinkled sky. Before your eyes a smokestack thrusts skywards. Thick, fatty smoke gushes out.

Sparks beyond count. Sparks scatter and flash across the starry sky, mingle with the stars, and you cannot tell whose light is the brighter.

Unnumbered naked bodies. Auschwitz under your bare feet. The column marches towards the smokestack.

Night about you. Auschwitz about you. Death holds your life between his hands — a circular mirror held up to your eyes. You

don't see Death in person — not yet. His face is hidden behind
the mirror. His breath alone blows on you, the way wind blows
on a spark in ashes —

The better to see it go out.

On both sides walk S.S. Germans, silhouettes of silence
mantled in night. You are no longer free to choose your own
death. You have already been handed over. Death, your master,
is taking you to his abode.

Walking under his long cloak, you scent his smell. You can no
longer change places with anyone. He knows your flesh by now.
He has seen you. Naked, you come unto him.

No longer are you free to choose your own death. This is —
Auschwitz. Already your feet tread the corridor of your death.
In a moment, you'll go inside and see him face to face; your lord
and master, Death-of-Auschwitz.

Hush. No one here dares breathe a word. Words are no more.
Sparks slip out of the smokestack. You squeeze the bit of soap
in your fist. Countless feet. Naked feet. You can't hear their steps.
Night leads you unto itself. Stars vanish over your head.
Nothing is yours anymore. Even your head's hair has been taken
away from you. This hair is still worth something, you are shorn
of all. Except for a single spark you still carry within you.
Death has bought it on the Jew-market. It belongs to him. Soon
it will shoot out of the smokestack.

Auschwitz.

What kind of factory has death established here? Of what
use to him can be the sparks leaping from the smokestack?

Inside

A network of pipes above your head. From the pipes jut
shower sprinklers. Row upon row of sprinklers. And in the
sprinklers — pores.

From somewhere in among the sprinklers, rusted opaque light
drains down, illuminating what is imminent.

The open gate thrusts into the night. Still they keep coming in, an unbroken stream: naked bodies. More and more. Human beings. All of them looking alike. More, still more.

It's getting packed. Bodies, nude and clammy, around you. Naked skin on naked skin. At each contact your body shudders. But as the shudder runs over you, you suddenly thrill to a feeling of reprieve. It wakens a sense of life in you. You still have a body! A body of your own. As if you had it thrust anew into your arms. Never did you love your body so. You feel: fear whetting knife-blades on it. Soon it must grapple with a faceless death. Soon death will make his appearance. Soon you will see him, face to face. He sits on high, inside the sprinkler pores. Any second now —

All eyes are fixed on the sprinkler-pores overhead.

The gates of the "Bath House" lock. Even night is no more.

Naked bodies enclose your body. Trembling, the way your body trembles. The tremor runs from end to end, like wind through cornstalks in a field. The ends you cannot see, but you can feel the shudder of all the bodies through your own. The gates are sealed. Even night is gone. Nothing but bodies. All bodies are now — your body, just as the death of any body is now — the death of your own.

Inch by inch all bodies turn to stone. A crust of hoarfrost jells over all. Petrified, all.

Necks.

Not a head to be seen. Not a face. Nothing but necks. Necks thrown back. A plateau of necks flung back. Headless.

To start with — a torso; on top of it — shoulders; on top of the shoulders — a neck. And atop the neck — pores. Dark pores.

Sprinkler-pores of the Auschwitz "Bath House."

Rust-clotted light eddies between the necks and the shower-pores. In this light, death hovers. About to swoop.

Necks like cobblestones. Death stomps upon them as on stones of a deserted street. Here he is all by himself. Here he is on his own grounds, alone. This is his abode. Here he casts off his veils and his face shows. Here, in the sealed "Bath House"; here, in this inner sanctum of the Temple of Auschwitz.

And you see him.

Heads flung back to the nape, like chickens' heads in the slaughterer's grip. Mouths wide open. Necks stretched out. To the slaughtering knife on high.

You see his face.

Death's face.

The necks take no breath.

Suddenly —

A wisp of white steam. Unhurrying. Leisurely. Lightly twisting and weaving. Gracefully curling against the sprinkler-pores as if circling a floor in dance. And gone.

The necks take no breath.

Then from the pores swell — drops. Single drops. Pendulous. Pear-shaped. Unfalling. Suspended above the eyes —

The necks take no breath. Petrified.

Suddenly:

Thin, scalding streaks, vapor-encoiled. White-hot whips. A moment — and off they break in mid-air. Gone.

Once again empty pores, dark and secretive. Shower-pores of the Auschwitz "Bath House."

Suddenly:

Thin, freezing streaks. Biting whips of frost. A moment — and off they break in mid-air. Gone.

Empty pores, dark and secretive. The shower-pores of the Auschwitz "Bath House."

Over again

again,

and again,

All at once a wailing shriek crashes out:

"Water! ! !"

"Water! ! !"

"Water! ! !"

Bodies leap up into the air, howling and screaming, tearing their scalps as they would tear hair. Drenched in tears they bawl out their happiness in wild uncontrollable weeping:

"W—a—t—er! ! !"

At the walls, fingers pinch their own body; raving mad they scratch and grovel at the blank walls: *Water! ! !*

As if corks had all at once blasted from their stoppered throats. All as one, they wail with twisted mouths, weeping and flailing arms gone crazy with joy:

"W—a—t—er! ! !"

One, the Know-it-all in every crowd, shouts back at them: "shut up! Of course it's water! That's all it is — water!"

But not one of them pays him any attention. The mouths sob at him, shrieking insanely: W—a—t—e—r! ! !

Until the gates unlock.

Outside, the night foams and bubbles with the mirthsome guffaws of SS Germans; it rolls on the waves of their laughter, breaking over black-horizoned shores. The Germans stand in the dark and look on, the way spectators watch a comedy enacted on a brightly-lit screen — and double up in laughter.

The naked bodies stream out, as if spewed onto an unfamiliar shore. Opposite them, the sparks stream from the smokestack and vanish over the starry sky. Stupefied, they stare at the laughing maws and do not understand —

They don't understand that truly happy were those who got, not water out of sprinklers, but Zyklon cans jetting blue gas into their lungs, instead.

They don't understand that truly happy were those who at the very threshold of Auschwitz were turned into these sparks now spraying out of the smokestack opposite —

W—a—t—e—r!

They are alive —

And they go marching, drunk with joy, towards the blocks of the camp called "Auschwitz."

Dawn in Auschwitz

Backs.

Backs and eyes —

In Auschwitz, everyone tries to draw his back as high up as he can, as if the back were a woolen blanket you could pull over your head to keep warm.

On the narrow backpath running along the blocks.

More than ten thousand shadow-men.

No beginning, no end to them. There is no beginning, no end in Auschwitz. Everywhere around, beyond the walls of barbed wire surrounding your camp, range more camps. No end of camps. Isolated from each other, like stars. A galaxy as yet beyond human ken and exploration. To the right — 'B' Camp, to the left — Quarantine Camp. Behind — Women's Camp. In front — the milky way, down which the packed vans roll without cease, without cease, to the crematorium.

And above all — the final hour.

The final hour of the night. Ten thousand pairs of eyes spill out of the blocks every day at this hour, the hour before dawn, into the backpath. Cleanliness. The German loves cleanliness, so now the block orderlies 'clean out' the blocks — they are apportioning out the bread rations. Instead of four, they'll cut eight and ten rations from each loaf. The loaves they gain in this way will soon be on their way to the latrine — the camp stock-exchange — to be traded for cigarettes for the Block Chiefs. Four cigarettes to the loaf. And outside, on the backpath running along the blocks, ten thousand and more shadow-men hop a hypnotic jangle dance, foot up, foot down —

The cold earth of Auschwitz sucks through the soles of bare feet the last remains of marrow from the bones.

Eyes —

A river, over which rain whips endlessly, trace enormous, gaping water-eyes. A stream which flows from the railroad platform to the crematorium. Ever the same stream, never the same drops. Drops ever changing, ever new. You see them in their sluggish, silent flow as they look at you with glass-sheened gazes, probing your face for some stir of their own lives which stream by — out of their reach — and see naught. Not even the camp they're passing through.

Eyes —

Eyes that for fifty years struck foundations for generations to come; and eyes of fifteen years, in first beauty of flowering, brimming with sap and vitality, finest of mankind, the crown of creation.

Eyes — of lords of wealth, ruthless tyrants of international trade-marts; and eyes of careworn shopkeepers, harassed and cowed, penniless tradesmen whose worries have been handed down to them at birth: where will food for the Sabbath come from? Who will pay the teacher's wages?

Eyes — of seekers, men of science, artists anointed with divine gifts of genius; and eyes of thick-tongued labourers, prayer-books clasped in blackened, calloused hands. Grey as the days of the week, nondescript as the chemicals fructifying our earth.

Eyes — of self-designated lordlings, society's upper crust, whose names by the clash of cymbals were always heralded; yet miserly, insatiable, enviously ill-willed if ever success shone in through another's window. And eyes of men of soul, delicate spirits, noble, modest — the sweet fragrance of our lives.

All along the road, from the Auschwitz railroad platform to the crematorium, these eyes all now beg the answer to one question:

When will the soup ration ever be handed out?

O Night-of-Auschwitz on backs and eyes!

Hour of awful despair and pity.

Enigma of an hour when night wraps in one black robe S.S. man and campling alike.

Far, far off, lights speed down the main road. You know: each pair of lights — a packed van heading for the crematorium. Many a time you have wished to be taken to the crematorium at night. Better by night than by day. At night you can cry.

Never did anyone weep on his way to the crematorium by day. At night, tears come from your eyes.

Awesome mystery of Night-of-Auschwitz, never to be fathomed by mortal man.

Until night is drawn from your lids, like black scabbard slipped from sword. Slowly the chill blade of Auschwitz day gleams bare.

To the west, the red bulbs still glow along the barbed wire — a coral necklace on the flesh of Auschwitz night.

To the east, the new day already shows ashen-grey among the block-roofs, as if the mounds of ash had quit their posts by the crematorium, falling into line here between one roof and the next.

The S.S. sentry climbs down the watchtower ladder, rung by rung: first, the black boots, then the rifle slung across back. He carries the night with him, folded and shrivelled. Like a black crow night roosts on his shoulder. He turns over his post to his *Kamerad,* the day-sentry, who climbs up the ladder, rung by rung: first the hands, white hands, soaking in the new day — your day. Every hunched-up back in Auschwitz now proffers your eyes your own loneliness. Each pair of eyes gazes at you with the pity for a life that once bore your name —

Dawn of Auschwitz on backs and eyes.

"Wiedergutmachung" *

I

My mother was — my mother.

How can I describe you, Mother?

My mother was the most beautiful of all mothers in the world.

My mother said:

"No! My little boy didn't do this naughty thing . . ." Lovingly she pressed the profiles of my head between her open palms, her fingers long and parted. Her eyes plumbed the depths of my

* In German, reparations, literally 'setting things aright.'

own as she said, "I! I did the naughty thing! Because I am my little boy!"

Afterwards, I was always very careful to behave, because I couldn't bear for my mother to do a naughty thing.

My mother!

Of all mothers in the world mine was the most beautiful.

On her way to the crematorium my mother saw my face. I know it. Because I, too, on my way to the crematorium, saw my mother's face.

Mother, now they want to give me money to make up for you.

I still can't figure how many German marks a burnt mother comes to.

"My little boy couldn't have done this naughty thing . . ."

Mother, I feel your open palms touching the profiles of my head. My eyes sink into yours: Isn't it true, Mother, you wouldn't take money for your little one, burnt?

II

My sister's hair was long and curly, the colour of ripe gold. Mother's hands vanished in white-gold foam every time she washed it. Whenever she rinsed it, sheer gold cascaded down my sister's nape like a waterfall all the way to the bottom of the tub.

My mother loved to plait ribbons into her tiny daughter's hair. She would sort them out, singing soft to herself as she did:

> "Ribbon green for hair's gold sheen,
> Ribbon pink for chocolate skin,
> Ribbon blue for the eyes . . ."

My sister's eyes were blue like sky.

Sabbath morning, in front of the house, when the sun met my sister's hair, neighbours at their windows would call:

"Whose hair is that, little Goldilocks?"

"My mother's," answered my sister.

I loved my sister's hair. She never lifted scissors to it. She said "My mother's" . . .

Before my sister was burned in the crematorium of Auschwitz they shaved off her hair. Seventeen years the golden locks lengthened on my sister's head. Long locks of gold. Seventeen years.

In a shipment of hair, in sacks, or in rectangular bales, tight-pressed like cotton from rich plantations, my sister's hair was sent to Germany. It was unloaded at a factory, to make:

> blankets —

> > soft club-chairs —

> > > upholstery —

Somewhere, in Germany, a young Fräulein now covers herself with a blanket. A single hair of gold, unprocessed, thrusts out of the blanket's weave. The Fräulein stretches out a bare arm, pulls, pulls . . .

"Fräulein! Give me back that hair! It's out of my sister's golden locks . . ."

My sister, now they want to give me money for you. But I don't know how many German marks your curls should bring.

"Whose hair is it, little Goldilocks?"

"My mother's . . ."

Mother, Mother, what do you say — how much is your little Goldilocks' hair worth?

My mother croons to herself:

> > "Ribbon green for hair's gold sheen,
> > Ribbon pink for chocolate skin,
> > Ribbon blue for the eyes . . ."

My sister had eyes like the blue sky.

III

Among tens of thousands of shoes I'd recognize a shoe of yours, Father!

Your heels were never crooked.

Father, your step was always straight.

Each day a new mountain of shoes piles up on the compound of the crematorium. Remember when I was little? The first time you let me shine your shoes, I polished them tops and bottoms. Oh how you laughed at me then!

"There is, sonny, a dirty side as well, on which a man must tread. When you're big you'll understand."

Father, I'm big now.

The sun bends over the slope of the tall shoe-mountain, illuminating it for me as with a flashlight:

Shoes!

Shoes without end!

A torn baby-shoe — like an infant's open mouth, eager for the full spoon in mother's hand; a torn baby-shoe — an infant's head, eyes bugging from the shoe-mountain to the sun shining on earth.

Nearby —

A narrow, delicate woman's shoe, high and slender-heeled, brown-scaled. Open on all sides. Several entwined leather straps on top. The gold imprint on the steep arch glitters in the face of the sun.

Nearby —

A lime-spattered workman's shoe. The sun peers into it as into the mouth of a cavern hacked into barren mountain rock.

Nearby —

A mountaineer's shoe, its toe wedged in the side of the mountain, as if the climber had paused in mid-ascent, breathless: "Oh, what a view! . . ."

Nearby —

A leg with a shoe on its foot — prosthesis to the groin. Trouser-less, naked to the sun.

Shoes!

Shoes beyond count!

Father, among tens of thousands of shoes I would recognize
yours!
Your heels were never crooked —
Father, your step was straight.

IV
How can I take money for my sister the "Field Whore" from
you — and not be a pimp?
Give me —
Give me back one single hair of my sister's golden curls!
Give me back one shoe of my father's;
A broken wheel from my little brother's skates;
And a mote of dust that on my mother rested —

(*Tr.* Nina De-Nur and Chayym Zeldis)

David Rokeah (1914-   )

DICE

The dice that my brother forgot
As he played in the street
I want to gather up
One by one.

Shall I stone the shadow
That does not return,
The silence that keeps secret
What happened to my brother
As he hunted the shadow
Through the night that betrayed him?

Do not smash the streetlamp
The only one in the street.
My brother will not return to the dice.
Go to the necromancer.
He lives in the cavern
And conjures up the dead.
Ask what is to be done with the dice
That my brother forgot
As he played in the street.

(*Tr.* Michael Bullock)

BLACK SAND

Voleanic islands hold
Your memory. Black sand sieves through
Its red, at sunset, a
Last jealousy of your sea.

Cast your net in the depth
And number your catch.

A fish with blue fins,
A many-pincered crab,
A lost engagement ring.

Gulls hide their eggs in black sand:
Night spreads its net over yours.

(*Tr.* Jon Silkin)

STORM

Gulls on the shrouds.
Listen how the lightning runs down the anchor chains
To the bottom of the sea.

Thunder on Carmel.
It echoes in the roots of cypresses,
In the ears of the caves.

(*Tr.* David Saraph)

SIEGE

The evening in Jerusalem is late to
Forget the warm words of the summer captive
Within the mountain clefts.
Smoky from burned-off weeds, time
Invests the body. The body images that
Enfold their jealousy in shadow, are

Invested by the battlements that circle as
A school of gulls laying siege to
The entrance of a port.

Night after night I go with the wind that
Blows from the sea to the wind that comes from
The caves which honeycomb the groundwork of
The wall.

Night after night your voice that questions the end-tellers
Fears the wind that speaks out from the earth
The magic letters on the cloister wall
Beyond the battlements.

(*Tr.* D. Saraph)

CIRCLE

I make no talk to
Explain the stubborn circlings of my thought
My likewise stubborn and capricious love
That does not know but love —
But I will tell what is
Between me and the pinetrees of Jerusalem
That makes the bluethorn glow in summer and
Turns the sea green.

(*Tr.* D. Saraph)

AND AFTER YOU

And after you —
The sea gnaws the shells of the night
Lights of boats bobbing dispersed along the skyline
Pebbles grind teeth
On the beach.

(*Tr.* D. Saraph)

THE FISHERMAN

The fisherman who gathers driftweed
From the sea
Will return to the sea
(A night with gouged out eyes
In his empty net)
His shadow floating like a shredded sail
Between night and day
Will see the last star
Quenched in the lonely observatory
On the mountain.

(Tr. Bernard Lewis)

WANDERER'S MORNING HOUR

Hour that never returns.
Footsteps lost in the desolate dark.
Your existence all in the balance
on this night, when having escaped
from the solitude of your room
and wandered through the market-places,
you put out the last streetlamp.

I said: I shall sell my dreams
to the traders who wake in the early morning
and put chestnuts on the fire in their stalls
for the new day.
But the mane of dreams, flaming
like longing,
did not move the fruit-sellers.
They asked: How much does the flesh weigh
that quivers under the mane?

You went to the windmill. Into its sails
morning flows in,

In the whirling of its wheel your dream dissolves.
Your hand that grasped
at the fleeing night
pledges its love to the sun.

(*Tr.* Michael Bullock)

BONFIRE

The clock stops its hands now.
And the sea;
Only the sea beats out
The pulsing of your fear.

The gulls abandon the cliffs
Used for keeping watch from,
Before the day, which
Drifted listlessly,
Has become evening.

Wanderer, prepare to feast;
And turn your back upon
The sea that waits for prey.

(*Tr.* Jon Silkin)

Abraham Birman (1923-)

ROUND PEGS IN SQUARE HOLES

I

Perspectives and rainbows encumber a mandrill,
Ignoring a chlorophyll-orphaned tendril.
Sunset, post-mortem, exhibits in scarlet
Divine equanimity, moonlit and starlit.
And liver-cells burgeon afresh in their haunt,
And nerve-cells just don't.

II

Scorpions strewn like discarded slippers
On dune and desert. Man-fearing skippers
Jettison bibles before they embark.
White lies fondle the greyness of liars,
Ants aspire to the rank of ant-lions,
And a clear head struggles alone in the dark.

STRANGE THOUGHTS
(In memory of Albert Einstein)

They still believe that if you try
To make a wish when you behold
A falling star across the sky
Your wish comes true, however bold.

A little boy in failing health
Would ask to frolic, jump and shout.
The rich men — to increase their wealth,
The wise — to quell some gnawing doubt.

But is there one who views the dark,
His throat gone dry, his eyelids swollen,
And murmurs at the last lone spark:
"I wish the star had never fallen"?

Aharon Amir (1923-)

THE OLD DOG WEEPS FOR HIS MASTER

today there was food on my plate
but the food had no taste
or else i couldn't swallow
without you i can't eat at all
without you my life isn't worth a bone

tomorrow i shan't find a thing on my plate
i feel you can't give me anything anymore
for they came and took you away
and you didn't even call me
and you didn't even fondle me
just went away and will never come back
never never never
i don't know why but i feel it
and when i feel i know

my tongue is lolling out as if it's hot today
but today it's cold

i breathe ah-ah as if back from a long long chase
chased indeed chased whom
i howl as if five big ones bit me all over
i wail for my master
my master
i shall go crazy
woooooooh!

i howl for my old age
for my old years i howl
don't i know i'm old and useless
the young dogs sniff once and go away
the bitches no longer wait for me to sniff
the little people no longer play with me
and the cats those lowdown cats won't even look at me

maybe i'll go wild like the wild dogs
who have no home at all
no house nothing to watch over
i'll live in the hills like a jackal
like a jackal
look around for carrion
for fallen birds or dead rats
and howl for my master
until i die
and when i die
i'll go to the place where he's gone
and he'll fondle me there

(*Tr.* A.B.)

NOTHINGNESS

I woke up at night and my language was gone
no sign of language no writing no alphabet
nor symbol nor word in any tongue

and raw was my fear — like the terror perhaps
of a man flung from a treetop far above the ground
a shipwrecked person on a tide-engulfed sandbank
a pilot whose parachute would not open
or the fear of a stone in a bottomless pit
and the fright was unvoiced unlettered unuttered
and inarticulate O how inarticulate
and I was alone in the dark
a non-I in the all-pervading gloom
with no grasp no leaning point
everything stripped of everything
and the sound was speechless and voiceless
and I was naught and nothing
without even a gibbet to hang onto
without a single peg to hang onto
and I no longer knew who or what I was —
and I was no more

(*Tr.* A.B.)

T. Carmi (1925-)

THE BRASS SERPENT

> *"And the LORD said unto Moses,*
> *make thee a fiery serpent and set*
> *it upon a pole: and it shall come*
> *to pass, that every one that is*
> *bitten, when he looketh upon it,*
> *shall live. And Moses made a serpent*
> *of brass . . ."*
>
> (*Numbers* 21:8)

> *"Three voices are there which are*
> *never lost . . . the voice of a woman*
> *in labour, when she mounts the*
> *chair of pain: that voice floats*
> *from end to end of the world: the*
> *voice of a man when his soul departs*
> *from his body: that voice floats from*
> *end to end of the world: the voice of*
> *a serpent when he sheds his skin . . ."*
>
> (from *The Book of Splendour,*
> Sefer Ha-Zohar)

I. *Till His Time Come*
He will hit at your heel.
You will hit at his head. He will stay
Still, he won't be ashamed to stay still.
You will blunder, in love, through the day.

Silently he will nest in the heart.
His truth shall whisper. You'll pry,
Morning and evening, alert,
For his track in the cracks of the lie.

He is happy to feed off dust.
Bullnecked and avid, each day,
You will feed between tombs of lust,
You will sing with the gongs of the sea; you will say

A threefold prayer to the strand
Of the three-phased moon; you will roar
For the sun of Gibeon to stand
Till you make your throat sore —

But he will hold his peace.
Death and lightning fill his voice. Yet, dumb,
Upon his belly he will pass,
Sheathing his swift sharpness.

Till his time come.

II. *On the Riverbanks*
Down to the riverbanks I went
To find if my flesh was in flower yet

To see if my hands were yet in flower
And if the lightning was back in my eyes.

To find if an echo replied to my voice
And if offspring had come to the rays of my moon

To see if the water explained my face
And my face could see the transparent answer.

Turncoat, I shrank from the bank of the river
And past me seeking the sea, it uncurled.

But the serpent took off his coat
And forever his voice floats free through the world.

III. *Vigils*

The dawn scatters dust in my eyes.
I am tired, very tired. The first light
Grieves for the charms desecrated at night.
Round and round the wheel of my Zodiac flies.

The noon, and faith broken in act and choice.
I am very tired. I chew the dust of the lie.
May my sycophantic mouth choke with dust, for my
Caverns hold neither a voice nor the hint of a voice.

The moon like a squinting lizard bobs at me.
I am tired, very tired. My bride, how shall we fly
Upon the belly of our frayed love: by
What miracle? And how can we be free

If we do not dare to lift our eyes to the power
That stands in the heart of the sky, serpent and flower?

IV. *He Shall Live*

Shape a fiery serpent with your hands.
Raise it upon a mast.
He on whom the snake has left his mark
Shall look upon it, and shall live.

And if his heart is empty,
And if he moves always in the dark,
The burnished one he shall see,
And his light shall flare, and he shall live.

And if he prays by day on what comes past,
And his dreams by night are of booty,

He shall look upon the calmness of the mast;
It shall calm his heart, and he shall live.

And if time corrupts his skin,
And the substance of his teeth crumbles fast,
He shall look upon the gleaming one,
And shall flower like the rod, and he shall live.

And if the dryness of his night breeds nothing,
And if sackcloth droops from his loin,
He shall look upon the piercing thing,
And his seed shall rise in all who live.

And if greed fills the slits of his eyes,
And the malice of his lust is his king,
He shall look upon the piled skins as they rise,
And his heart shall grow wide, and he shall live.

And if his laughter brushed the Law away,
And if arrogance flashes in his eyes,
He shall look upon the dragon's coils all day,
And shall fear in his heart, and he shall live.

And if the sound road is his road,
And if his actions take the right way,
He shall look upon him who is crooked,
And the road shall lurch away, and he shall live.

And if he casts no shadow at his feet,
And is mocked, and his body is not echoed,
He shall look to the voice that is afloat
And is free, and he shall see, and he shall live.

And if it is delayed, the song of his desire,
And his illness is hope, and he must wait,
He shall look upon the rings of fire,
And be wedded in the eyes of all who live.

And if his day is burnt as with brands
And his flesh howls to heaven for love,
He shall look to where the burning seraph stands,
He shall look upon the creature of his hands.

And he shall see it and shall live.

V. *The Serpent Speaks*

They say the serpent is the subtlest beast.
Look up at me,
Exposed to your eyes upon a mast
And kinsman to your pain:
As explicit as the tall wheel of the sun.

I smuggled pain into the womb, they say.
Barren woman, raise your eyes to me.
If I slashed you with my eyes, or if I twined,
Miracle's pennant, round your nudity,
Your issue would be more than wind.

I marred man's flesh with thorns of sweat, they say.
My ruined one, look up at me.
Tell your thanks, for if the scorpion of dream
Or the pride of the leviathan had fled
From your heart, you would be as good as dead.

They call me the eater of dirt, the crawler, the kneeless.
Yes.
But have you seen, in the spring,
My chrysalis burst into the miracle
Of a seraph's wing?
Restless ones, look up at me.
You will flower, you will flower.

Not by riddles, not by those, but by what you see above,
I shall tempt you to live.

VI. *The Man Speaks*

I know the serpent has unsheathed himself
Like a sword, and dressed in light, like the Spring,
I know the seraph has spread like the dazzle of the sun
A burning wing.
How can I raise my human eyes to him?

I know that whoever dares to raise his eyes
He will save.
I know that now he is crying aloud,
O burnished and cold, O kingdom of sleep and the wave —
How can I not be ashamed to look at him nude?

I know further that my fingers are scaly,
Reptilian, old. I know that the rod
Of the reeking serpent once flowered within the wall
Of the tabernacle of God.
What would I do with my hands if they flowered and dew
    fell?

I know that the people see the mountain and the holy
    voices.
But already they buy and sell the cast skins
Of the serpent. I know that the plague will only
Come to the people again.
Am I strong enough to be like a leper and lonely?

I look. I look. My eyes,
Nervous reptilian heads, draw in
And out, grubbing for darkness from above.
I look, and it is the earth at which I am looking.
I feel my blood flowing.

VII. *Miriam*

From brass did Moses shape a serpent

Miriam, Miriam, dancer and sister
To the sea and the high tide of the drum
By my side like a living well
Rise, rise.
Teach me to bless the portent,
The morning light of the gazelle,
And the terror of my eyes.

Upon a mast did Moses raise the serpent

Miriam, Miriam, prophetess and sister
To murder, flower and snake,
Teach me to conceal what I can,
To reveal myself, a striking seraph, and to raise
My hands to the tabernacle of the whitening snow
Like one who prays.

If a serpent had stung any man

Miriam, Miriam, leper and sister
To spittle, to shame,
Teach me to be
Like one dead, outside the camp.
Teach me to speak truthfully.
Teach me to raise my eyes:

Who beheld the brazen serpent did not die.

(Tr. Dom Moraes)

WORDS TO A SORCERESS

I can't remember this: I can't keep track.
Autumn pounced at me on my homeward way.
I shed my hands, leaf-light and very quietly,
And my inquiring voice did not come back.

Flails fell, and I was scattered, as chaff flies.
My shadow sneaked away from my front door.
My eyes deserted me, flying to the shore.
She had snared my neck from far with lovely eyes.

A sign, give me a sign. But don't unmask
Too much. Perhaps I am too late in this place —
I can't remember much, so do not ask —

For still the pool of water holds my face.
Through the ring of whisperers reach towards me, console
Me. Your voice, folding me, will make me whole.

(Tr. Dom Moraes)

BUILDING SITE

On the tiers of the scaffolding, there are no fears
For the start. Night hums through us on crossing wings.
Distances in the palm are wakeful things:
"Tomorrow: or next year: or countless years . . ."

At a ladder's foot, the drowsing watchman dreams:
A door, a ceiling, curtains and a bell:
In the meantime, the water-meter still
Waits to be fished up from the streams.

Pull your hand, please, back out of night, and place
Infinities of dishevelled surmises where
My hand is: and an eternity of hair
In the moon. The tiers are lovely now. And yet,
Where, I wonder, and how, shall I shield your face
On the great day when the building is complete?

(Tr. Dom Moraes)

EVEN IF SHE SLEEPS

Even if she sleeps, her hand will still emerge
From sleep, aware, more than the surgeon's hand,
Of odour, breath, and pulse: and understand
The distant whisper of the hidden dirge.

Even if she sleeps, her ear is open still
To the clang of cold metal and the heavy stir
Of an eyelid. All the wakefulness in her
Waits for the strange bewildered calm to fall.

Even if she sleeps a little, still she keeps
Watch on leaf-fall and the awkward hurry of Spring,
On the next one who will die, and each living thing.
Peace to her dream. She sleeps:

But her skilled hand will still chop surgically
At living flesh, until the end of day.

(*Tr.* Dom Moraes)

WHEN SHE WENT OFF

When she went off she trusted it to me
(Or left it with me as a gift perhaps)
This bitch, expectancy,
Which battens on the words of gate and bell,
And the vine rustling at the sill.

The night (lie still!)
Stands tall, unmoving, empty of her steps.

Ssshh! My sweet bitch, it's not my fault, you see,
(My keeper's services are honorary)
That tongues of rust saw at the gate, that all
The leaves like hailstones fall.
Come here, my beauty. Here to me, I say,

Muzzled, of course,
And from your jowls I'll wipe the froth away.

(*Tr.* Dom Moraes)

AWAKENING

Please pass your hand across my lips.
I'm not accustomed to this light.

Batlike our love in flight bangs round through dark.
It does not miss its mark: and your face shapes
My hands for me. What shall I learn in light?
Quick, pass your hand across me.

Your childhood (what's the time?) slept in my arms.
It's ten o'clock between the sea and night:
Midnight between us: seven between the blinds —
Oh no, I'm not accustomed to this light

Which comes to make cold slits of both my eyes,
Opening like gunsights. On those scales I weigh
My blind eyes, and the terror of your clay.
Quick, pass your hand through me.

Face to face, I'll have no face, perhaps.
Perhaps I'll stay quiet, or perhaps I'll talk.
Please pass your hand across my lips.
I'm not accustomed to this light.

(*Tr.* Dom Moraes)

TO A POMEGRANATE TREE

Get away from here, get away.
Go visit other eyes.
I wrote about you yesterday.

Green, I said
To your branches bowing in the wind
And red red red
To the still drops of your fruit
And I brought your root to light,
Your moist, dark, stubborn root.

So now you don't exist.
Now you block off the day,
And the yet unrisen moon.

Come, my love, and see
(I wrote about you day before yesterday
And your young memory
Afflicts my hands like a nettle).
Have a look at this odd tree:
His blood's in my eyes, on my hands, on my head
And he still stands where he stood.

(*Tr.* Dom Moraes)

Haim Gouri (1923-)

SONGS OF FRIENDSHIP
(excerpts)

II

When the world was created in legend and myth
God bestowed on each of us humans a present:
Iron sturdiness on the smith,
Calloused hands and a prayer on the peasant.

The sheen of dinárs He gave to the merchant,
Insight to the sagacious,
Subtle fingers to the surgeon,
Long breath to the pearl-fishers.

To the builder — a mind that soars skyward,
Sheer perseverance to the masons,
The heart of a bat to the loving and wayward,
Attraction to loadstones and maidens.

He gave to the mothers a brow bright and clear,
A curse to the barren jades,
A taste of salt to our sweat and tears,
A burden to backs and shoulder-blades.

To our flesh — the hunger of martens,
To our scars — a date of restitution;
Dauntless faith to the martyrs,
Memories to destitution.

To traitors — a tenure of treason,
To haters — wrath and adherence;
Forgivers were given a merciful season,
Avengers were barred from forbearance.

Fear He gave to the sated,
The starved were endowed with hatred.

Drunkenness fell to the wine and spirit,
Delusion to the wise,
Bloodshed to cannon and turret,
To the duped — an open pair of eyes.

The ends He gave to the tepid,
The starts to the intrepid.

Between the roses and the thorns,
To bold inversion giving birth,
The law of opposites adorns
The story of our lives on earth
That flow and strive and forge ahead
Between the feather and the lead.

VIII

Envy has many faces,
And smell and colour.
Her sparks fly up to interstellar spaces,
Her paths are far too numerous to follow.

Some envies' lives are rich, full-blooded, lush
With banquets, hangovers, misgivings.
Some thrive in edifices decked with plush,
Some weep alone, unbidden, in the bivvies.

Some eye each other closely, pert and vile
Like rival concubines behind a wall.
Some hasten off to dip their pens in bile
And scorch the paper like a living coal.

There is an envy, too, that trips or hustles,
That silently pursues its secret ends.
She is the wood-worm mouldering the castle,
She is the knife that severs friend from friend.

She flips her kisses with a vampire's wings,
Her plans into a spider's web are woven.
She smiles demurely, as a scorpion stings,
Beatitudes by quiet curses cloven.

Her chic and glory, advertised in fairs,
Consume familiar hearts like acid burns.
How many totter on her creaking stairs
And tumble headlong, never to return!

(Tr. A.B.)

IN THE CAVE

Bare walls. So bluish is the silence
That frugally into the dampness dips.
Alone, unheeded, far above the pylons,
The annals of the cavern drip and drip.

These pillars were not strenuously quarried
Or posited by operation crews:
No, patience built them in the dark, unhurried,
A handiwork of Nature in recluse.

Stone-flowers stare opaquely at the ceiling
And shimmer in the darkness, droplet-born,
Against the light that walks on all-fours, stealing
Through manikins of moss and tangled fern.

(Tr. A.B.)

REQUIESCAT

In memory of H.B.D.

Lay wreaths upon the stone. Wreaths
About his amazed, listening face arrange.
He was yours, but you were like strangers:
With no ray of light on the cobwebs in the eaves.
And he looks at you out of mist, curtains of rain.

From childhood the picture of his face rises
To my memory innocent, aglisten.
Blue youth heated the iron of his life,
Struck by the fire from the pupils of his eyes.
And as a man, he came to anguish and cognition.

But what happened between his walls was mute,
And what outside of them was choked —
To the conflagration of his nights he took.
And with his best friends did not lock
What he carried to his grave and to his book.

This is the book of facts. Like a cruel scroll
His heart and his confessions on my deafness strike.
I beg pardon for the grudge that passes by,
For the error that repeats eternally,
But he just smiled to me from beyond his life.

(*Tr.* Ruth Finer-Mintz)

ODYSSEUS

And when he returned to his birthplace he found sea
And various fishes and grass floating on slow waves
And sun weakened in the rims of the sky.

An error forever recurs, said Odysseus in his tired heart
And returned to the crossroads close to the neighbouring city
To find the road to his birthplace that was not water.

A wayfarer weary as a dreamer yearning much
Between people who spoke another Greek.
The words he had taken as provision for his travels had mean-
　　while perished.

For a moment he thought he had slumbered many days
And had returned to people who were not amazed to see him
And did not open their eyes wide.

He questioned them with motions and they tried to understand
　　him
From the distances.
The scarlet turned violet and went in the rims of those skies.

The adults arose and took the children standing about him in a
　　circle
And drew them away.
And light after light yellowed in house after house.

The dew came and fell upon his head.
The wind came and kissed his lips.
Water came and washed his feet like old Eruoclyea.
And it did not see the scar and continued down the slope like
　　water.

(Tr. Ruth Finer-Mintz)

HIS MOTHER

Long ago at the end of Deborah's song
I heard the silence of Sisera's chariots that were late.
I looked at Sisera's mother gazing through the window there,
A woman with a streak of silver in her hair.

"A spoil of varicoloured embroidery,
Of varicoloured embroidered cloths on the captive's neck,"*
　　maidens saw.
He lay as if asleep in the tent then.
His hands were very empty.
Traces of milk, butter and blood on his chin.

* Judges 5:30.

The silence lay unbroken by horse or chariot.
The maidens kept silent one by one.
My silence touched their own.
After a while the sun went down,
The setting rays went out.

For forty years the land was stilled, forty years
Horses did not race. Dead riders did not pierce with glassy eyes.
But she died, shortly after her son was killed.

(*Tr.* Ruth Finer-Mintz)

FLATTERING THE VULTURES

Vultures have no sense of fatigue.
They are strong and steady birds.

They are not too friendly.
They don't inhabit roofs;
No answer at call. They cannot be bribed
To peck in squares flooded with pigeons,
Or alight quivering on your shoulder.

Vultures have no sense of fatigue.

They wake to soar again,
After a spell, they return to soaring,
Moving black and slow across the wound of heaven.

They are still flying there with me, the vultures.

(*Tr.* Dov Vardi)

Nathan Zakh (1930-)

FROM YEAR TO YEAR THIS

From year to year this gets more subtle,
It will be so subtle in the end, —
She said, meaning just this.

But time and again I can feel I am drowning in Time,
I feel I have been drowning a long time.
He stopped.

All this is because you are sinking, she told him.
All this is because you are sinking, you know.

I don't. At times I think my strength is failing me.
Subtle, you know, is a term for negative.

I know and I congratulate you on your find.
I congratulate you on the colour of your eyes,
There's nothing you ever leave behind.

This exactly is what worries me,
This exactly is what mourns me,
This exactly is what I feel.

Wrong again: you're fit and fitness is surrounding you.
It's all around, it lifts you shoulder-high,
If you are patient enough it'll even embrace you,
Finally, it will just have to kiss you.
You know how these things come about.

(*Tr.* Richard Flint)

A MOMENT

A moment of silence please. Please. I
Want to say something. He walked
Right by me. I could have touched
The edge of his coat. I didn't. Who
Could have known what I didn't know.

The sand stuck to his clothes. In his beard
Was a tangle of twigs. The night before
He must have slept alone in a barn. Who
Could have known that in another night he'd be
Empty as a bird, hard as a stone?

I couldn't have known. I'm not blaming
Him. At times I feel him getting
Up in his sleep, moonstruck as the sea, saying
To me: My son.
My son. I didn't know you were that much with me.

(*Tr.* Richard Flint)

REPENTANCE

When they told me to repent
I was no longer able to repent.
I have gone too far, I said to myself
And to them, to be able to repent.

I cannot come back, the dead man said.
The worms do not allow me to repent
And the odour of the earth fills my nostrils.

All that lives lives, said he who lives.
But listen, brothers, don't dread the dead.
He will never again
Be able to repent.

(*Tr*. Richard Flint)

AN ACCURATE ACCOUNT OF THE MUSIC SAUL LISTENED TO IN THE BIBLE

Saul listens to Music.
Saul listens.
What Music is it Saul listens to?
Saul listens to Music
That recuperates him.
Saul listens to Music.
It's Music he listens to.
And the people about him are gone, as if
They have vanished, everyone dumb.
For Saul listens to Music.
Is this the Music
Saul should listen to
As times go?
Yes, this is the Music that Saul
Should listen to as times go
For there is no other now
And perhaps there will be none
Till Mount Gilboa.*

(*Tr*. Meir Wieseltier)

---

* It was on Mount Gilboa that King Saul was defeated by the Philistines. At the end of the battle he fell on his sword and died.

MISTAKEN

He is alone. Therefore it can be said
without a tinge of doubt. He is mistaken.

When I chanced into town I feared
that I should have to go begging.
No. I came to him. He stood there. He was mistaken.

Rain covered the distance between sky and earth
rather reluctantly.
I thought there would be frost that night.
He asked me what. I told him.
He looked at me sadly. Shook his head. No. He was mistaken.

When I rose to go he saw me to the door.
He did not try to hold me. Didn't delay me.
I looked at him. Extended my hand. He took it. No.
He was mistaken.

(*Tr.* A.B.)

FOR PHIDIA

Come evening I put the mask down and placed it
in the corner to dry until morning. I could not
say, but I find it difficult to sleep on stone. Maybe
I'm asking too much on critical days like these,
but at night I have no wish to veil my face. I hear
my hands performing in the darkness. Not a pianist with
his well-trained fingers. A poet with a florid
painted face. Of course he tells it to the boys all night long.
He says "for Phidia," viewing the mountains. He is awake,
the light in the window's still on, they listen how he storms;
he says "for Phidia" and they take this for an image,
looking around the room to find the real thing, but
they are still young, their faces bright, in the dark
they cannot see the storyteller's face, they cannot see

how wide awake he is, how he sneaks a smile
behind his beard, teases his creator, apologizes, says
he cannot remember, tries to shift the blame, but as he repeats
"for Phidia" he stops, starts to look at his hands
like a mountain, a moment of silence, it occurs to him he's a
    desert, his tale
seems suddenly complete, like a dream, finished. Then he is
    bewildered
but at once agrees.

(Tr. Meir Wieseltier)

WHAT WAY

What way my love has gone. Summer is
Fleeting. Any fleeting breeze remembers better than I
What way, what way my love has gone. Meanwhile I sit
In a café, working out a crossword. The radio
Is on. Upon the twig something hops,
Trips and skips again. What way,
What way has she gone. Disappeared. Meanwhile
I am here. On my trousers appear
Bits of ashes. The forebrain chatters while the eyes
Focus as usual on silly girls. Assiduously
I roll memories like chestnuts in a game. What way,
What way. All is erased. In an emergency
There is always myself. So near me
That I can almost touch it with my hand
That's drawing meaningless birds
And stillborn lizards
On a sheet of paper
I've just found in my briefcase,
Off a writing-pad I took from the publisher.

(Tr. Meir Wieseltier)

SERGEANT WEISS

An everlasting flower
Buds on your forehead.
Your cheeks nurture
Unseen grubs. Rarely
Is your name mentioned
Except on manoeuvres. You move
Through your flesh as though
Through a sieve; my time is still
Troubled by your hand
Whose watch marks time
Other than my own.

Until your arrival I
Had thought it necessary
To hurry back to my task.

I don't know how you treat children now.
It is hard thinking of your face
When I am afraid. Events have moved on
As to a late reel of film
That may not be watched again.
In the desert, still, they
Worship you, with their boots on.
The brambles bend themselves
Down, remembering your orders.

Weiss, I do not know
How much time will pass
Before I recall you,
Suddenly restless.

Your way was right, perhaps.
In the house you have built
Nothing presses itself on you
Except cold, heat, hunger,
Desire perhaps. Water will

Not prosper round your eyes.
The oleander will
Not sing through your tongue. Mother is dead;
You will not be a child again, Weiss.

In this continuing parody on people's fate
War manages one of its most convincing roles:
Formed by the formless, it can hardly recognize
Its image; surrounding you like a sea that pierces
The swimmer's flesh, rearing the waves. Your madness is
One of war's possibilities, not the worst.
You created a situation we must put up with.

In the delusions that leave no sign of their existence
But move in us, I see your eyes agape, sometimes,
Like oases. We who were not able in these years
To shape the war into a thing we understand
Remember you as a page written in lines close together
Hard to read, correct; spaces of time passed, not fulfilled.

(*Tr.* A.B. and Jon Silkin)

CHIEF WORM

Forgive me, chief worm,
If I didn't salute your sisters,
The second-rate worm and the third.

It was my intention to do so
But the glow-worm, mind you, the glow-worm
Snatched half my desire from my hands.

I hope to fulfil my intention tonight.
I do not know of any other night
On which I could fulfil my intention.

Remember me as I was, your admirer.
Sometimes I think I followed your lantern
For a few nights, but as from now

A deeper darkness will envelop me, no doubt.
I am not afraid, chief worm,
Of a deeper darkness.

(*Tr.* A.B.)

Yehudah Amikhai (1924-   )

O GOD OF COMPASSION*

Of God of Compassion —
If God weren't so full of compassion
the world could have some of it too.

I who gathered flowers at the foot of the mountain,
who gazed steadfastly at all the valleys,
who brought fallen bodies down from the hills,
can swear that the world is devoid of compassion.

I who was salt-king on the seashore,
who stood irresolutely at my window,
who counted the footsteps of angels,
whose heart lifted heavy weights of pain
in those fearful contests,

I who employ but a fractional part
of the words in the dictionary,
I who solve riddles whether I like it or not,
know that if God weren't so full of compassion
the world could have some of it too.

(*Tr.* A.B.)

* These are the opening words of the Jewish prayer for the dead
(*El Maléy Rahamim*).

THE VISIT OF THE QUEEN OF SHEBA

I. *Preparations for the Journey*
Restlessly
like a zebra
the Queen of Sheba
rose from her lair
amid stifled curses,
clapped her hands.
Maids fell askew,
bats changed vigils.
On a strip of sand,
with her bare toe, she drew
a fancied picture
of Solomon, like
a bearded pike,
a nebulous fixture,
half-man, half-pigeon.

The Master
of Ceremonies
brought too many caskets,
too many peacocks.
She opens her own
collar bone
so that Solomon is
able to smell her heart.
She also brings feathers
to tickle his ear
for a merry start
when they will laugh together
between hiccups.
She knows, with some precision,
about circumcision.
Her avid curiosity

blooms with leprosity.
Her blood's sisters scream orgies
amplified through her organs.
The sky
neglects to button its fly.
Her head is the hyphen
of her eye-paint.
All the harlot-houses
of her lymphatic
zest lit up
with red carouses.
Emphatic
turmoil in her setup
raged full blast
till at last
night came, hotter and hotter,
like an old teeter-totter.
Infernal night.
Eternal night.

II. *The Ship At Anchor*
A ship lying at anchor.
A ship white with languor.

A ship laden with longings,
some pent-up, some thronging.

A ship slippery and narrow,
no libido in its marrow.

Among the masts there perches
one of the Queen's own kerchiefs,

woven from the gossamer
of birds whom this awesome earth

killed before nightfall.
Yet it was rightful

for a white ship to dance
cheek-to-cheek with the quay, and prance

between the prenotions of wave and sand
till morning overtook the land.

III. *The Morn They Left Sheba*
She called her thighs back together
while her mood was already a
zebra of opposite shades.
In her body's oven the heart
rotated on a roasting-spit. The morning howled.
A torrid rain poured down.

The manacled forecasters prognosticated.
The engineers of her somnolence
came riding on tired dromedaries.
The gudgeons of her laughter scurried away
before the rising shark of her wrath.
Cowardly corals hastened to hide in her armpits.
On her belly appeared traces of nocturnal lizards.

She sat up in bed, sharpening riddles for
masterminds, like colour pencils. From
old men's beards an African apron
was made for her, while her secrets
were embroidered on silk napkins.
But lions still upheld the laws
like the Tablets on holy Arks,
on the whole wide world.

IV. *The Voyage Through the Red Sea*
Fish exhaled through the water,
through the long wait. Skippers
navigated by her yearnings' map, by
her belly's rings. Her nipples
accosted her like undercover men.
Her hairs exchanged whispers like conspirators.

In dark corners between sea and dolphin
the counting was quietly begun.
A solitary bird chirped amidst
the constant warbling of her blood. Rules
dropped out of textbooks. Clouds were
ripped to shreds like treaties. At noon
she dreamt about intercourse in the white snow,
about yolk and the pleasures of yellow wax.
The air rushed to enter her lungs. The mariners
babbled in piscatory gobbledygook.

But under the world, under the sea,
cantillation reigned supreme:
Everyone chanted everyone.

V. *King Solomon Is Waiting*
Never any rain.
Never a drop of rain.
Always a nebulous fixture,
always a husky love.

The wild-goose-chasers
were back from the pasture.
In the courts of the world
stone-flowers blossomed,
dedicated to alien gods.
Trembling ladders dreamt
about those who were
dreaming about them.

Yet he saw
the world's lining
torn slightly open.
Yet he was wakeful
like so many stables
in Meggiddo.

Never a drop of rain,
never a drop of rain.
Always a husky love.
Always a quarry.

VI. *The Queen Enters the Hall*
The rose of her blind pudenda
doubled by the mirror-floor. Redundant

was his caution while he rocked
on the throne and judged his flock.

Then he lay back on the couch
and rolled up his life's map to vouch

that he, a deposed and haunted vagrant,
sensed in the mirror a carnal fragrance

from above and below, as in a card-game.
And his blood began to play a hard game.

And his face changed seasons like a vista
till he reached the end of his twisted

mind. Then he grew a little
wiser and knew that her soul fitted

the supple body he was to embrace.
Like violin, like violin-case.

VII. *The Duel of Riddles*
In the ping-pong of questions and answers
no sound was heard
save 'PING-PONG,'
the counsellors' cough,
sharp tearing of paper.
He made black billows in his beard
to drown her speech.
She turned her hair into a jungle

for him to stray in it.

Words were set down with a clang
like chessmen.
Tall-masted thoughts
overreached one another.
Empty jigsaws filled out
like stellar vacuities.
Secret hoards were exhumed,
buckles and vows undone.
Ruthless religions
were tickled
and laughed horribly.
Her tongue fell over his
in the final game.
Maps were pinpointed on the table.
Everything was open, poignant,
pitiless.

VIII. *The Empty Hall*
No word-games
were returned to their boxes.
No box was shut
when the game was over.

Sawdust of quizzes,
nutshells of parables,
woolly stuffing for
delicate riddles.

Coarse burlap for
love and contrivance.
Cast-off conundrums
rustling in the litter.

Long-winded problems
wound on a spool,
miracles thrust into cages,
chess-knights forced back into stalls.

Empty crates
(*'Handle with care!'*)
empty crates
sang hymns and anthems.

Then the king's guards marched upon her
and she fled, dejected,
like a swarthy snake
in the withered grass.

An indulgent moon circled the towers
as it did on the Eve of Atonement.
Caravans set out unmanned, uncamelled,
went voicelessly on and on and on.

(Tr. A.B.)

WHAT IMPELLED JOSEPH

What impelled Joseph to tell dreams
Stops my tongue.

What lulls a child to sleep in its cradle
Keeps me awake like fire.

What rouses and rages and rips an oak tree in winter
Drives me inward like a fist.

The great portal opened wide for you
Blocks my road as if it were a plug.

(Tr. Dov Vardi)

ELEGY ON A LOST BOY

I know how high the water rose last winter, but I do not know
how high love rose in me. Perhaps it overflowed. What remained
on the walls of the *wadi?* Only congealed mud.
And what remained on my face? not even the thin white line

that lingers on the child's lips when he has drunk his milk
and set the glass with a clang upon the bright marble.
What remained? Perhaps a leafy mark in the little stone
put on the window-sill to watch over us like a guardian angel
when we were inside. But to love is *not* to remain, not to
leave a mark but to change entirely, to be forgotten.
To understand is to bloom. Spring understands. To recall
your beloved is to forgo all wealth, to forget other loves,
to shut other doors. Look, we have secured a place, laid a
coat or a book on the vacant seat, vacant perhaps forever.
How long can we keep it? Someone is bound to come. A stranger
will sit there and make you turn round to the door with the
red legend and glance at your watch. This too is a habit
that grew out of prayer like a kiss or a bow. And outdoors
new thoughts are always invented. They too are donned by tired
human faces like many-coloured lanterns. Or look at the child
whose thoughts are painted on its face as on ware for others
to see — he cannot as yet think for himself. The earth
is travelling fast, under our soles like a revolving stage, like
your face which I thought was mine but was not. But the boy
got lost. A last scion of his games, a darling son of his
building-bricks, a grandson of his ancient hideouts, he wandered
with his pealing toys into the midst of empty wells after the
Holy Days, in the terrible cycle of cries and muteness, in the
process of hope-death-hope. Everyone joined in the search.
Everyone was glad to peep into never-never land. Loud voices.
A low-flying plane steeped in meditation. Police-dogs with faces
like those of philosophers. Question-words hopping on thin legs
in the drying grass under our very eyes. Trite expressions from
prayers, talks, newspapers. Jeremiah's prophecies on all-fours.

And the streets of the city, clogged with demonstrators, thumped
like the heart of a sick patient. The dead were already clinging
like bunches of ever-ripe fruit in the world's annals. Those who

looked for the boy found lovers in hiding, antique jars, all that
desired to remain hidden. Love was too short to cover them all.
A head or a pair of feet protruded into the wind when the cool
night came. Or they found a short-cut of sharp pain instead of
the long, forgetful streets of prolonged satiation. At night
there were the names of foreign cities, dark lanes, nations
long extinct. They were like the name of my love. She raised
her head and listened. Had someone called? No. But the boy
had disappeared, and lanes stood out on the distant mountain.
There was little time. The olive-trees bespoke hard pebbles.
In the great fright between earth and sky new houses grew.
Window-panes cooled brows on a sultry night. The wind rose
from the wizened grass like a beast of prey. The unwittingness
of mutual recourse erected high bridges in the desert. Traps
were laid, reflectors switched on, nets spread in warps and woofs.
The searches went on and nobody saw that the boy was hiding
in houses of tomorrow. Eternal paper, printed and unprinted,
rustled between feet. Orders rang out. Numbers were specific:
not 10 or 50 or 100 but twenty-seven, thirty-one, forty-three
so that we should be believed.

At dawn the search was resumed. Quick, quick, I've seen him
among his well-toys, his stone-games, his olive-pebbles. I heard
his heartbeats under the rock. He's here, he's there. Did you see?
The trees moved a little. New shouts, an ancient sea bringing
new ships to a foreign port. We got back to our cities where
a sizeable sorrow was allocated at appropriate intervals, like so
many letter-boxes. The stones sang in a choir of black mouths
into the earth, but only the boy heard them. He was already
an old-timer, played hide-and-seek with clouds, befriended
olive-trees, rubbed shoulders with routine and change. He left
no trace, just like love. He belonged completely. For to love
is *not* to remain, is to be forgotten. But God remembers, God
returns to our little room to recall how he once wanted to build

His world on love. Nor has He forgotten our names. Names are
never forgotten. When we dust with an old blouse we still
call it a blouse. How long? We change, but the names remain.

Everyone ignores the names, the rules of the game, the hollow
shouts. An hour passes. Hair is being cut in the barber's shop.
The door opens. It is thrown to the sweeper's care. The barber's
watch is near your ear when he bends over. This too is time.
Perhaps the end of time. And the boy has not been found.
Corrugated voices ring out in the surging wind. We went to
bed together. I got up and left the room. She remained there,
her eyes agape with fear. She sat up, leaning on her elbows.
The sheet was white as doomsday. She had to go into the world
that started at her threshold. But the boy stayed on and began
to look like the mountains and the winds and the trunks.
A family throwback indeed: the face of a youth who has fallen
in the Negev re-appears in the face of his cousin who is born
in New York. The break of an Aravah peak shows in the face
of a broken friend. Ridge and night, fancy and tradition.
A night habit grown into a lovers' rule. Temporary precautions
deemed permanent. Police, shouts outside. The fire-engines
do not come back tearing and shrieking. Quietly they return from
ashes and cinders. Quietly we too return from the valley,
from love and search in retrospect, unheeded but still heeding.
We thought someone cried out. We opened our earlobes with the
palms of our hands, enhanced our hearts with love so that
we could hear well and forget better

                                        but the boy died at night,
clean, well-combed, licked into mortal shape by the tongues
of God and dusk. "When we arrived there was still light, now
darkness prevails." Smooth and white as a sheet of paper in
an envelope, sealed and sung in the psalms of the dead's domain.
Some of us went on searching, looking for pain or joy compatible
with their laughter. Not every two entities are compatible. Even

the hands belong to another body. Yet we thought we heard
something drop to the ground like a coin. We halted, turned,
bent over, found nothing. Then each of us went his own way.

(*Tr.* A.B.)

A GIRL NAMED SARAH

Sarah writes her letters
ruthlessly, by sea-mail.

For her lovely eyes
she has to pay indemnities
throughout her life.

Under the canopies of her eyebrows
constant weddings are held.

Her mouth grew red in the forest,
Along with my childhood.

In her room the world, packed up
in trunks, is ready for the move.

She likes love's unleavened bread,
all agog to set out
through desert and wilderness
for the Promised Land.

I would like to talk to her
about changes in my life's map.

(*Tr.* A.B.)

YOUNG DAVID

After the outburst of the first few hails
Young David went back to the waiting boys.
Already those who clattered their hard mails
Were so disarmingly mature and poised.

They formed the usual shoulder-slapping queue.
Some swore, some spat, laughed hoarsely, even cheered.
But David stood alone. Henceforth he knew
There could not be another David here.

And suddenly he wondered where to put
Goliath's head that his numb hands were yet,
Through sheer inertness, holding by the curls.

Now it was heavy and superfluous. Birds
Who flew into the bloodshot distance heard
No longer, as he did, the shouts and snarls.

(*Tr.* A.B.)

TOO MANY

Too many olives in the valley,
Too many stones down the slope.
Too many dead, too little earth
to cover them all.
I must go back to the landscapes
Painted on banknotes,
To my father's image on the coins.

Too many memorial days, too little
Remembrance. My friends have forgotten
The lessons of their youth.
In a secret nook lies my beloved
And I am left out, a prey to the winds.
Too much lassitude, too few eyes
To contain it. Too many watches,
Too little time. Too many oaths
Taken on the Bible. Too many roads,
Too few ways to one's fate.
Too many runaway hopes.
Too many dreamers, too few dreams

That can reverse the course of history
Like the dreams of Pharaoh.

My life is closing behind me. I am left
Outside, a dog to the blind, cruel gale
That keeps prodding me in the back.
Domesticated, I sit on my haunches and wait
To lead her through the streets and alleys
Of what could have been my real life.

(*Tr.* A.B.)

TO THE WOMAN
(excerpts)

IV

All night long your shoes shrieked
At the foot of your bed.

Your right hand is dangling from your dream.
Your hair is memorizing its nightly lesson
From the wind's tattered textbook.

The rustling curtains
Are envoys of foreign powers.

V

When you open your coat
I have to double my love.

If you are wearing the white round hat
I have to accelerate my blood.

In the room where you love
The furniture must be cleared away.

All the trees and mountains and seas
Must be evicted from this narrow world.

VI

The heavily chained moon
Is silent outside.

Caught in the olive grove
It cannot disentangle itself.

The moon of rounded hopes
Is rolling among the clouds.

VII

When you are smiling
All serious notions grow tired.

The night mountains are silent by your side,
The morning sand goes with you to the seashore.

When you do good things for me
All the heavy industries close down.

(*Tr.* A.B.)

David Avidan (1934-   )

MEGAOVERTONE, ANOTHER WAVE

At a certain dishonourable moment you find it agreeable to think
    of yourself
as of a gradually expanding earthquake
on some remote island, surrounded
by a surprisingly calm ocean, almost benevolent
in its malevolent curiosity.
You return, though through a late reincarnation, to an old habit
of addressing yourself in the Second Person,
trusting to an immediate response.
At this intimate moment it is pointless, of course,
to be engaged in purely aesthetic tasks.
The poetic language, as such,
will, in any case, occupy you
at some of the other moments, after partly surviving
the present situation that will be described henceforth,
for the sake of your sanity in the first place, at dictation speed.
At this very moment, however, you would like to give up

David Avidan

all your aesthetic advantages, in order to conceive disciplin-
arily
the earthquake which continues to expand,
as mentioned above.
Yet you realize only too well that you are self-disciplined
rather than self-discipled,
and that the difference between these two
may equal the difference between just-now
and just-a-moment.
Instead of disciplinarily conceiving the situation, you stick to
your habit of bewitching yourself with words
that lost their magic power over you
years ago,
when some of your very early signals
were perhaps received elsewhere.
Now, long after the still wind
had rubbed off those signals with an indifferent thumb-wave,
strewing them, with some disgust,
among fractured sunrays,
that overfamiliar nightmarish redemption
lands on you, for a brief gracious moment,
like, say, some spaceship from another solar system.
A divine light illuminates, all at once, not only you, but also
the whole island, all this unnecessary piece of land,
and for an instant you may even imagine that within minutes
you'll practically take off together with
this miraculous supervehicle that has landed on you,
and will actually take off thanks to your existence alone.
But no.
The take-off takes place without you, as usual,
abandoning you completely,
together with all you do or do not possess,
turning you into the same remote waste-island as before,
too anxious even to decode someday
what and to what it keeps signalling,

until the surrounding alien water
floods, with a solemn rustle,
the last unreceived signal.
Yet this water retreats of course after a while,
becoming reflective and hospitable like a mirror.
The still wind is considering possible moves in alternative
    directions,
and even a fullsized pigeon,
carrying in her mouth an olive leaf pluckt off,
flies noiselessly above the evaporating ground,
hopelessly looking for some ark,
or at least a scrap of an ark, for a momentary landing,
in order to proclaim perhaps, at a summitrivial moment,
a close yet hampered redemption.
But don't despair.
The dry desert, mind you, is still very much alive.
Down there, in the bowels of the earth, the armed forces
start getting reorganized.
The cleft island's crust breathes placidly,
with about the same placidity, accompanied by the tension of
    liquid curiosity
now noticeable in the rerising water, charging up above the
    oceanwaves' shoulders,
witnessing, with hostile amusement, how a sole sniper,
one of your own men, snipes down
the silent pigeon at the terrible altitude,
with a single shot, an admirable precision
and a distant spasmodic pain,
realizing, with a clarity-beyond-terror,
that even this isn't the last error.

(*Tr.* by the author)

EXPERIMENTS IN HYSTERIA

Some people have nothing to lose, some people
have nothing. What
haven't they? What
haven't some people to lose? Some people
are carrying a time-bomb, carrying
a time bound to blow up. What
is still binding them up? What
are they up against next? And there are, of course,
other techniques of phrasing the sensation. One can, for instance,
slow down, all at once, the flow of reflexes, so that suddenly
everything is recrystallized. They look,
they who have nothing to lose, they look, they are being looked
    at,
they may even be looked at, as if in the form of a supermodern
        submarine, a water-vehicle
yet untried, never to be tried. The deep water
inhales it with a trembling sigh. This is
its greatest moment. It has no
objection to the speed, it has no
alternative speed to offer. Yet it's clear
that this isn't the thing, for the thing is:
will the bulkheads hold or won't they hold? Surely,
surely they'll hold. Fortune-tellers, the best of them,
have no doubts about it, that is they may have their suspicions,
    but
the best of them, the skilfullest ones, have no doubts. So this is
    the thing:
Will they hold? Won't they hold? And the more important
    question, one which
can, of course, most unnecessarily though feasibly, always
        feasibly,
be expressed by high-octane metaphors, the most vital

question, the supra-vital one, is as follows: Am I, all of a sudden
in the First Person, so as not
to be misunderstood, am I
already afraid or still afraid, already
afraid or still already
afraid?
It is therefore imperative to stick to writing. No
missing of chances is permissible. Perpetuate yourself while
there is still time, before time stands still. Later you'll change,
    later
it will be too late. Later
it is always late. This is
the method, the only one. There is of course an alternative, but
it will be tried, definitely tried, only later, only
when it's too late. Come, come with me. Summer
will never return. The ground
is already on the move. Later
I shall take you to the circus. In there
everything will be on the move. The whole surface of the earth
will shift slowly, with pathetic effort, with full
responsibility. Never again will
a more responsible shift take place. Come, come
to the sudden happiness. Remember me at my best, remention
me at my best on another morning, when I shall re-awake
into the murderous, morbid rhythm of registered impressions
to which I seem irremediably addicted.

                                    (*Tr.* by the author)

KAS BUVO — TAI NEBUS*

Two ex-Lithuanians, who remember
their mother-tongue even more vaguely

* A Lithuanian proverb which means 'What has happened will never
happen again.'

than they remember their mothers, meet
in a café on a fine cool evening, and exchange
memories. Say, how do you say *past* in Lithuanian? Indeed,
how do you say it? Embarrassing. Pretty Embarrassing.
     Perhaps
there is someone in this pleasing area, within
a radius of two miles or so, who can
fix this trying lingual short-circuit. But
it gets very late, and all those Lithuanians
who aren't dead will be fast asleep.

How do you say 'sleep' in Lithuanian?

(Tr. by the author)

SUMMER NINETEEN SIXTY TWO
(Blueprint for a Cool Filmscript)

A man signals greetings to a woman.
A woman signals greetings to a man.
Half the world signals greetings
to the other half.
A hasty, almost intangible moment of concentration, then
     everything
begins to move, falls into two Indian files, marks time.
The sun marches in the middle, on parade, without turning
right or left, without favouring either file
with an aura of empathy, mention, promotion. It rolls on
with suspicious alacrity, groaning
like a red wild boar, riddled by African spears, though
still undetached.
A moment of misunderstanding. What
will come of it? Will something
come of it? Will someone
come of it?
Initiative, hidden deep in the facial furrows, refuses

to enlist, evinces
dangerous pacifistic proclivities. Only towards the end
does it consider capitulation. A 'yes, but' expression on the
faraway faces.
Yes but, yes but, yes but. But
is it for me? Is it for you?
Can you rival my *amour propre?* Can you
match your *amour propre?* Can we
match? A close moment. A close
shave. The stylish murderer
sharpens a photogenic razor on his victim's necktie. With sur-
prising elegance
he provokes the necktight rope that has waited for him
since early youth. He entertains. He reaps
applause. Humor, American style. It dribbles
quickly, avidly, heavily, like tropical rain,
on the distant sounds of a children's church-choir, attempts
to re-evaporate before reaching the ground, yet seeps into it
with a desperate whine. Now is the time
to remember again, during a hasty, almost intangible moment of
concentration,
the vaguely-defined rules of the game. Our skilful fingers on the
typewriter are
a glorious fountainhead of kinetic energy. They have
every resource with which to destroy the world. The world
has every resource with which to be destroyed by them, extin-
guished by a kiss. We have
finally come to the kiss, to the long-sought confirmation. The
atmosphere
is a charming camouflage-net, spread leisurely on open perils. It
calls for
frequent sacrifices, unconfined to the artistic domain. It forces
the precious issue in order to turn once and for all, once but not
for all, into
something else, into something more. Now is the time

to forget again, anew, once but not for all, the rules
of the game. We have survived
another winter. We only live
from summer to summer. The elaborate delusion
of gradual interseasonal progress is
our best means of defence. How many places, after all,
can still offer such a wonderful sun as the
Mediterranean Basin? The more so because
we came here by dint of a primal decree that can't
be commuted or confuted. We refile it
every summer, in a summary manner. And there is
water, sun and water, water and sun, water and water. In the
     beginning
there was water, and the spirit of God hovered over the water,
     and in the end
there will be water, and the spirit of God will hover over the
     water, and as long
as the world has more water than nonwater, more
sun than nonsun, it is still permissible
to look forward calmly, with relative leisureliness, to the forth-
     coming
generation. Now
something must move on, must effect
that inevitable egress without which there is
no artistry and no rejuvenation. In this spirit
the stranger walks away deep into the long avenue that will
never terminate. A man
signals greetings to a woman. A woman
signals greetings to a man. Half
the world is suddenly parting
from the other half. Moreover:
the red wild boar, riddled by African spears,
has recovered with astounding speed and returned
to his proper place. Remarkable: he
did it again.

                                        (*Tr.* A.B.)

THE DESERT GENERATION

Let fear break through.

Brave solemn armadillos break through the sated grass
to have a look at the first and last sun in their lives.
Better than you can they realize the meaning of a chance.
This chance is theirs.

Let fear break through.

Let it break through you in short cool volleys, let it
tear you to bits, then cool down.
It will do so long before you break up.
This is its chance — your own, too.

Let fear break through.

You realize only too well you're part of the desert generation.
You can read this sordid discovery in the eyes of children
wandering around those bright streets which your father
      might have built and which
you, with some luck, may someday destroy.
The real thing will happen only when you're gone, only
      when you're gone.

Let fear break through.

You who were made to negate the world,
you whose only vouchsafe may lie in negation,
have caught yourself in flagrante delicto:
you have taken pity.

Let fear break through.

Await it patiently and courageously. Prepare
a cunning ambush. Give it
erroneous chances. Never
trust it. Do not fall asleep. Do not

love sleep lest you fall
into poverty.

Let fear break through.

Let it enjoy slow progress, like a desert army.
Let it march within you, like fear in the desert.
You realize you are part of the desert generation, yet very
    soon
you may hear a voice, a daring voice in the desert,
a voice tearing the sated grass to small burnt shreds.

Let fear break through.

For man is a plant of the field,
and you too are a plant of the field.
Do not assault fear in the field,
for this is the wish of the wind.

Let fear break through.

Soon you'll forget all the words,
all the words you have ever evoked.
Night will walk past you like an orderly,
dark and efficient, efficient and dark,
inside a burning hospital, within
some remote battlefront in which you never
fought nor were given a chance.

Let fear break through.

The morning will resemble all other mornings,
all other mornings and all other deserts.
Fear will break through, even though you won't let it,
and the desert generation will aim
very high.

                              (*Tr.* by the author)

TERRIBLE GRANNY
(An Affairy Tale)

Somewhere else I've pointed out that
the fairy-tale of Red Ridinghood is essentially
a story for adults, a definite case
of statutory rape. Yet
a further possibility I overlooked is the most terrible
of all. The wolf, mind you, the wolf
is in a diabolic fix. Let us assume, coldbloodedly but
not without full aesthetic awareness, that the wolf —
having bungled the role of grandmother — suddenly
became a grandmother himself, powerless
to pull himself out of the mess. Assume? It has
happened. "Come to me, come to me," venomously
     whispered
Grandma-wolf to little Red Ridinghood, shutting
her decrepit old ears to the howling wolf-pack, capped
with white head-dresses, collapsing on snowy tundras,
     covered
with sugar-powder. "Come to me. Come to me. By my side,
     dearest,
you can stay a virgin forever."

Undeniably a horrific possibility, not to mention
the Lesbian innuendoes. Still, it isn't clear
for whom the danger is greater: for the wolf or for
marvellous, footloose Red Ridinghood who managed
to transmogrify the dirtiest mind yet not lose
one single berry of those she had picked
in the magic, predictable forest.

(Tr. by the author)

SPANISH MUSIC IN WINTER

First Listening

Ten, nine,
eight, seven,
six, five,
four, three,
two, one. It has begun. It's
already inside, irremediably poured into the blood, setting in
    motion
a rapid weathervane within the skullbox, flooding
the nerve-centers with urgent transmissions, demanding
exact reports on reactions, exact reactions on reports, an impera-
    tive
state of oblivion.
A remarkable effect indeed. We have tried most pills, but
this isn't it. This is something totally different. This requires
    prompt
analysis. Where is the lancet? Where is the lancet? A thin
    matador,
with immobile eyes, has already turned it into a sabre. Old
    gipsy-women
have packed the children in ancient potsherds. A yellow Great
    Dane
assaulted a black cat that crossed his path diagonally. Black hats
and bright eyes were filled with blood. At that very moment
the heroic husband was horned by his wife, and then
the mad bull's horns gored him. Garcia Lorca
was watching him through republican field-glasses from a distant
    veranda. Too bad, too bad,
he commented sadly. Now, precisely now one must change the
    colour of water,
the wings of the raven, the regulations of liberty. For a moment
a reddish floor-cloth covered the whole world, the shouts, the
    weary eyes

closed under it. And then the castanets
chased fear back to its kennel, like a dog, one might say, since
     no other
domestic animal is equally suitable. Of course, the castanets,
the castanets. How could we have overlooked
the castanets?

Castanets

Toro motoro,
deliver and get.
Toro motoro,
you won't forget.
You'll cross the rivero
in a jungle boat,
and a black warrioro
will cut your throat.
Toro motoro,
no compromise now
between *bravo toro*
and the cow.
Between *bravo toro*
y el matadoro,
the highly-skilled warrior and the low.

Second Listening

Olé. All yea. All no. No. He who is getting old and slow
will rush away in a swift airplane. The snow
has already covered the scene of disaster. A long arm
spread black beads on it with
a masterful gesture. We have
nothing to lose. Urgency
is dominating us. Sex
is submitting to a foreign rhythm. A strip of fire
is consuming, kangaroo-like, jungle after jungle, lad after lad,

lady after lad. Was it good, was it bad?
Was it exactly like mamma said?
Europe is ageing. All its hope
lies in the Pelviterranean Basin, the new course, the new
intercourse, the long unyielding summer, the small
dark Italians conquering America in narrow beds after
a backbreaking workday. How,
how was it, Marcello? How the hell has he
picked up that chassis? Now
let us return at long last to the point. It's cold. Summer
sends postcards too seldom. It has nothing
to report. It wishes to export
itself to another planet while
there's still time. The bull is frightened,
the bull is pushing the earth backwards, he
belongs to the avantgarde. Something
will happen this very evening, precisely
under the strict discipline of
the castanets. How could we have
so long overlooked
the castanets?

More Castanets

Toro motoro,
relax, relax.
You'll come no moro
out of sex.
Toro motoro,
you are afraid
to stay out of dooro
before it's too late.
Never be fairo
with your fellow-mate,
for he won't sharo

with you your fate.
You won't be fairo
and he won't sharo—
so drop dead together, tête-à-tête.

Third Listening

Olé. All yea. All no. Here goes the snow. Now
all is lost. Nothing will revive. The phoenix
is much too fond of the sand. What use has it got
for thin atmosphere, windgust, inconsistent sun, essential
rains?
The drying river carries small pebbles into the sea, assisted by
winds
that have severed all family connections. The hills
are forming up in couples, like breasts, developing
dangerous wishes. The ground
is anxious to be ripped open. The sea
is skeptical. In the meantime
it digests atomic submarines with
digestants. It throws up
too often. The earth
is so willing,
so full of aplomb
for the Bomb.

All The Castanets

Toro motoro,
play it with ease.
Today or tomorrow
all will cease.
All will get doloro
beneath the depths,
and there will no moro
be a collapse.

Toro motoro,
when will you recall
the distant coloro
of the end of it all?
When will you restoro
the distant coloro
that you'll never again recall?

         (*Tr.* by the author)

A CLEAN MISS

Alone into the night? Alone
into this humid night? Alone
into this tapering night? A hundred lonely steps
will take you to the nearest square. And then
I'll join you of my own badwill, with dimmed lights,
with no motor-horns, no honourable intentions, not
a single signal.
In this fading-in forest grow eight traffic-lights, watered
by fitful drizzles, shedding
before springtime ripe policemen's hats, dictating
the rhythm of mobility. You're a kitten, a little kitten, a wet
little witch riding on a hoover toward highflown windows,
    blending
delectable poisons under picturesque awnings, purring
charming refusals in a low engine-lingo, remembering
the date of payment.
I could of course put you up, warm you
with an electric heater, dry you up
against my thermostatic body, bestow on you
a gradual, meticulous happiness till
morning, that inevitable morning, till sunrise, that
efficient, cocksure sun, peeling
pampered youngishness off male heads. The manly hair that
    vanished

overnight wanders off, as if by some morbid mistake,
settling back on human females' skin like a farce, like
a warning-signal to females-to-come, to females-
to-come-to. They try to exorcize it
with spells and incantations unknown to their foremothers, yet
it cries out, whines, scratches our youthful shoulders, insists
on its right to self-determination, reminds us
of birthdays, of inevitable
evolution.
It is high time to admit that we need, badly need
a proper, undisturbed place to shout in, a place
to shout and howl in, just
a place. In the meantime
we are already wearing a new toga, bright new
Roman sandals, wielding a heavy lance, alertly awaiting
the dazzling light, the lucid buzz
of a flying saucer, the poignant touch
of alien hands upon our overstrained brain-centers. Alone
into the morning? Alone
into this desiccated morning? Alone
into this crucial morning? A thousand social steps
will take me to the coming dusk, and then
you'll join me of your own freewill, with full distant headlights,
with a whole system of motor-horns, equipped with
strictly dishonourable intentions and
overfamiliar signals that I
shall no longer be able to decode.

(Tr. A.B.)

VEGETATIVE LOVE

The Theoretical Offer

Come to me, come to me, said the tree.
Grip hard. Forget everything.
There are love-cracks in my trunk. I am experienced. I shall
    learn.

My roots will embrace your hips. My leaves will enfold you.
I shall evict all the birds and monkeys.
I am yours, all yours.
Give me a chance. You are
going to like me.
I shall be obedient.
There is room for you at the top, the top that will come down
to you over the years. Learn to like it. There is more to it
than certain women. Sex is not everything,
when everything's said and done. Forget the world,
the skinsoft soundwaves, the boring temperature
of your cooling body, the liquids straining through you
from all directions, to all directions, the eyecolours,
the transient hair, the music, the hostile sea, the roads.
Stay where you are. Do not move.
Soon I shall introduce you to the bowels of the earth,
the depths of fire, burning from a distance my roots that long
for you, the dark and solitary waters following it
like hungry hyenas, the scalding kernel
of this enormous fruit.
Be my friend. Give me credit. You know
too much about women to reject me. Do not refuse.
Do not be flesh. Do not smile at me. Do not speak
prettified words.
I want your gravity, not your memories.
I have time. Think of me. Travel. Go round the world, float
in the deepening dusk, break away, lock the gates. Come back to
    me
in the damp darkness, in the still wind, upon the dust that
    trembles
for your sake.

Refrain

I don't know yet, said the man.
You will grow up yet, said the tree.
I have my doubts, said the man.
I have my answers, said the tree.
I'm itinerant, said the man.
I am eternal, said the tree.
There's radioactivity, said the man.
There is chlorophyll, said the tree.
The sun is cooling, said the man.
The earth's core is not, said the tree.
The earthcore too, said the man.
I have means, said the tree.
You're dangerous, said the man.
I am everpresent, said the tree.
I've heard of you, said the man.
You have heard *me*, said the tree.
It deserves some reflection, said the man.
Don't rush into action, said the tree.

Time Dimension

It is good to have you back, said the tree.
I have no means of contact. I cannot
grasp you at a distance.
I have examined every possibility. I shall keep my word.
I shall do my utmost for you.
You still fear me. You have too much
of that kind of death which frightens me,
too little of the kind you really need. You are juvenile.
You have suckled the milk of she-wolves, diluted with legends
in which I was but a tremulous backdrop. I am
more than that. I am yours.
Generations of mammals have passed by me in ever-diminishing

caravans. My fathers made way for them in empathic
scorn. They knew you would come to me
of your own free will.

Refrain

I haven't returned yet, said the man.
You have not matured yet, said the tree.
You're ornamental, said the man.
I'm that as well, said the tree.
There are others yet, said the man.
None that concern you, said the tree.
It will all change, said the man.
Together with you, said the tree.
I must contemplate, said the man.
I amply compensate, said the tree.
I shall voyage afar, said the man.
If you manage to start, said the tree.

The Practical Offer

Now you are here, said the tree.
I have nothing more to offer you.
You are skin and bone, kin and bone, sin and bone.
Together we can vanish at the right moment.
I shall abridge my life
for your sake.
Come to me, come to me, grip me hard.
Soon the silent saw will come and adapt
my measurements to yours.
Break with your frigid blood. Do not hold onto it
despite its will. Be proud.
My sap will spring after it.
There will be
no understanding between these two.
Whoever commingles them

has made a bad bargain.
Now I really do not know
what to say to you. The saw
has already touched me in the right place.
Lie there and wait for me.
I shall come to you with
the last of the nails.

Refrain

You are too haughty, said the man.
Don't be too cautious, said the tree.
You are mistaken, said the man.
Your pride is shaken, said the tree.
I shall forget, said the man.
How far will you get, said the tree.
I shall try and endure, said the man.
You are far from secure, said the tree.

The Counteroffer

Come to me, come to me, said the man.
Grip hard. Break slowly.
There are hate-cracks in my face. I'm gaining experience. I shall
    teach.
My legs will embrace your trunk. My hair will grow into you.
I shall summon all the flies and worms.
You're mine, all mine.
Give yourself a chance. I'm
going to like you.
Be obedient.
I've a line of thought for you, a thought that will encompass
you over the hours, like a cobra. Sex is everything,
before everything's said and done. I shall arouse you. I shall
    bring you

the skinsoft soundwaves, the changing temperature
of my invigorated body, the liquids streaming through me
and you, from me to you, to you and out
from various directions, from certain directions, the eyecolours,
the recurring hair, the music, the friendly sea, the roads.
Don't stay still. Move.
Soon I shall introduce you to the surface of the earth,
the alien fire burning at close quarters my limbs that long
for you, the wondrously organized waters following it
like a veteran army, the soft blushing shell
of this ripe fruit.
I'll be your friend. I'll give you credit. You know
too little about humans to reject me. Don't refuse.
Don't be chlorophyll. Don't vegetate into me. Tell me
prettier words than the ones I own.
I want your memories, not your gravity.
I have no time. Don't think of me. I shall travel, go round the
    world, float
in the dazzling light. I shall not break away. I shall not lock the
    gates. I shall come back
in the dryness of light, in the blowing wind, in the dust that
    uproots you.

Refrain

You have disappointed me, said the tree.
Your love has anointed me, said the man.
Without you it's the end, said the tree.
But not for your friends, said the man.
I have lost you at length, said the tree.
You have given me strength, said the man.
Another time, then, said the tree.
In the wind's decline, then, said the man.

(*Tr.* Richard Flint)

LOLITA

A Pep-Pill, to Snap into the Right Beat

A smooth nape is better
than a downy one.
A smooth nape scatters
new scents in town.
New scents are blended
with winter rain.
Warm words will run
into smooth napes again.
Besides, one should never ask
silly questions, please.
Someone may make it his task
to call the police.
And then, as usual, it might
end badly for all:
frankly, how can a tiger fight
against a patrol?

The Psychiatric Report

It is hard to determine how you got it. At first you spotted
a nightmare gone and come, come and gone, till it was thrown
over you like a butterfly-net. You listened to pop-records, space-
cast
from another solar system. It was so late in the day, that your
whole system
was fully conditioned to start afresh, the hard way. Palm-branches
beckoned to you, with familiar code-gestures, that you could
come rightaway. You
are a hundred, two hundred. Your daughter is twenty-two,
abundant
in fertilization. You are still within the boundaries of civilization,
paying duties,

litigating in local courts with a beauty grown oldish in your bed.
   You are full of yourself,
but they made a fool of you. Black cyclamens stalk you on the
   trottoir. You are
successful with kittens and puppies. The new disaster is still
   wrapped in nappies, but
she, man, she is already trying to grasp you, and will soon clasp
   you with hands
so pellucid that none will see you, that none will see her. Better
   spare
the idea of bed. Forget the techniques you adopted in those
   years whose vicissitudes
moulded your traditional manliness, when you accustomed your
   surroundings, with tolerant graduality,
to what seemed your personal originality, but was no more than
chronic inadaptability to gain a well-timed control over Time.
   Her
you must take in a different way, so late in the day, when there's
   but a different way. You are
a hundred, two hundred years. Your teeth are all here. There's a
   distant gleam in your gaze.
Maintain your dignity. Maintain your craze.
No humour, please. These, these
are the years good and nice. Commit every vice, and remember
that your death lies in wait. It has already made
up its mind, it keeps you on its sights. She is light. She might
be the best you've ever had. You'll be as good as dead
in her grip. She will be the trip
that will help you get high again, while your thoughts thread
round a bed, round a shed, round
a white elk galloping, despite all instructions, on a jet-black
snow, singing snow, playing snow, self-accompanying snow,
   clinging
with clenched feet to the marvellous hoofs beating a narrow yet
   compelling path
for your successors.

Inviting a Girl to a Matinee

Lolita Tallita,
shall I come today?
You haven't yet brought me
red ribbons, she'll say.
You haven't yet bought me
a bungalow black.
Lolita Tallita,
won't you call back?
How has it transpired,
without sign or speech,
that some girl expired
right there on the beach?
Some girl expired
in a bungalow black.
As quick as a fire
the cops will attack.
Lolita Tallita,
who made a vow
to hit, sly and bitter,
at both of us now?
Lolita Tallita,
I'll buy you instead
two ribbons, Lolita,
black and red.

A Sudden Ring from the Beyond

Tiredness is the prerogative of the wakeful. The complete
sexual avantgarde is off for its daily siesta. The arms are akimbo,
    the feet
drive away in an ancient chariot, harnessed to well-trained
    fingers. The eyes are shut neat
in accordance with all the rules of relaxation. Now, little by little,
    it happens. From

the phone-receiver there emerge, with effortless grace, two
    Smallitas. No need to guide them — they
know most of it anyway. They take up their place
beneath the earlobes. They have
small nimble tongues. They whisper
in shrill voices, like an accelerated tape-recorder, the
truth, the whole truth, nothing but the truth. The terrible
    wilderness
between forehead and toetips is responding. Gulliver,
Gulliver. A pink rain
seeps through, unremittingly, all of a sudden. Reliable fore-
    casters,
equipped with transparent lifebuoys, swim quickly along and
    across. Soon
the sea, the prodigious sea, will come up to it. Mythical monsters
will dash out with recalcitrant roars, with no consideration for
chronological priorities. This isn't anthropology. No, no, this is
the very thing, the thing itself, in all its astounding dimen-
    sionality. You can
die of it, you can be petrified by it, you can lose your senses,
    but you cannot
use your senses. Hence the inevitable conclusion: now, little
    by little,
it is over. Into the phone-receiver creep, with graceful effort,
    two Goblitas, mounted
on rare matchsticks manufactured in Hong-Kong. They most
    definitely have
slanting eyes. They have already wolfed down all the rice, all
the beautiful white rice. They will come
again tomorrow.

A Pep-Pill, to Snap out of the all too Right Beat

It's plenty of fun
going to school,
but in the long run
it's not real cool.
No girl should cram
for her final exam.
And yet, since it is
much too hot for a while,
let's play it with ease
and stay out of style.
And when we are finally out of the pinch,
we'll decide:
referendum or cool plain lynch.

Methodical Comment

Now, after so many digressions, it is high time
to hint, however briefly, at the *leitmotif* of the tiger, occurring
at the beginning of this poem and, equally if not primarily,
in other poems, earlier ones. Well,
we don't mean the old bespectacled tiger, nor
the young autumn tiger, nor
any tangible tiger. But can we help it if this banal
beast is so fascinating? It is, in fact, the only one
qualified to retain some of the tenets of poetical thematics
    which
we have so laboriously assembled during the past ten years.
    Therefore,
despite some stiff principles consolidated by our adamant self
    for itself, by itself,
in those years that weren't yet the best years of our life, we shall
    enable

our synthetic tiger to express itself to the best of its ability and
    present
mood — first with a touch of levity, then
with a touch of graveness.

Song of the Light Tiger

I haven't a mom,
I haven't a pop,
I've only a taste
for whitelk chops.
I've only a taste
for much too much
that somebody says
I mustn't touch.
So I spend my days
looking for trouble.
She-tigers I chase
at the bloody double.
And yet, on the whole,
though often in gripe,
I'm what you might call
a positive type.
It's also true
that if I pull through,
I shan't be a tiger
any longer,
but swap my smudges
right away,
and cops and judges
won't be in my way.
But in the meantime
I wait and wait
for lightning to strike
before it's too late,

to strike hard and sure
at the beatenest place
and make me secure
in what I've to face.
And then, and then
I could try, at least,
not to be tiger,
bloodthirsty beast.

Song of the Grave Tiger

Where, where does the jungle end? Where,
where does the summer start? Where, where is the autumn
located?
All these questions, together and apart, are
harassing him, harassing him unabated.
He tries to overcome them by dint of habit, with the aid of
preponderance,
with the help of common sense, yet he knows, how well he
knows, that the answer
regarding the jungle lies exactly where the jungle
ends, that the answer about summer is there for all to see, exactly
where summer begins, and that there is no autumn in existence
except
where autumn exists. Physical advantage and poetry, especially
the latter, are
of no use in this case, Hence, of course, the conscious renunci-
ation
of vast aesthetic possibilities, latent in this very poem and
suggested, for instance, in the first two lines with the intentionally
pedestrian
structure. And yet —
where, where does the jungle end? Sometimes, when the lungs
are filled with that rare kind of oxygen which we
inhale in moments of an exquisitely distilled despair, it seems
to us, it is clear to us, that we can conquer the world, that
nothing

is too difficult, too baffling, too distant or too
complicated. Sometimes
when the lungs, sometimes
when the oxygen, sometimes
when despair. But now it is
autumn, an autumn different than the one we sought, a con-
ventional autumn, one might say,
winter, grey light, almost Joycean, in short — illumination we
don't
relish, being a summer-animal mottled with grudges, abounding
in
introvertive roars, whetting
prosthetic fangs upon black basalt. All that is black, including
shirts, excluding women's hair,˙ enchants us, hence
the colour-restraint, typical of our verbal pattern. All that is
black, except
the light-track. And we are waiting, tense, relaxedly tense, wait-
ing-relaxedly-tense,
for the uncommunicated shock, the uncommunicating shock, the
uncoming shock that will
indubitably come. And we are tensely relaxed, relaxedly tense
for it, and we have audacity fractured in our eyes, and we
dispense with
the power of concentration, with the virtuosity of the roar and
perhaps, in the last analysis, with
the unceasing rutting-season. Only let it come, let it come, let
it come,
from above, from below, from within, with no limitation of
direction, rhythm, time or
colour or sound. And we take into account the pain, the physical
hazards, even
the tangible, immediate danger to the present structure of our
sheltered ego, not to mention
the change in our faces, the range of our shoulderspread, the
records

of roars we've already brought out, the deferred revenge-reckon-
ings, and the absolute
departure from here. But where, where? Anyway, what is there
to imply Lolita? And when
will it all end? Well, it will
end when it will. Till then
everything moves within the ken
of rhythm dictated by the old
bespectacled tiger and by the young
autumn-tiger, ranking of course among his successors, and also
by the certain brain-arbitrariness of the formulator of these lines
    who decided,
after due deliberation, to exempt wonderful, independent
Lolita-Tallita from the duty of obedience, and consequently
from the duty-of-combined-conclusion in this particular case.

(*Tr.* A.B.)

SONG

The soldiers asked a cigarette, a cigarette.
The woodlegs marched on sulphur, wearing skates.
Wood to wood. Spark to spark. And then a voice
was mildly introducing a dead choice:
"If nothing turns up now, my dear men,
we shall advance into defeat again."

(*Tr.* by the author)

PRELIMINARY CHALLENGE

An elderly couple bent over their cold supper, viewing
the dry wind with two pairs of moist eyes, awaiting
Death who is expecting
me.
Today I managed, at long last, to take off four pounds, after
five days of culpable negligence, and I'm perfectly ready

for the preliminary signs. Everything becomes
so frightening, yet so mollifying, when the
preliminary, not imaginary, signs have replaced
the dilatory disaster, when petty warfare has forever
procrastinated
the final battle.
I think a great deal about Death. When one thinks of him,
he relaxes, watches from a distance. He has some highly
developed
narcissistic qualities. Hence the interplay and interdepen-
dence between us.
He likes attention, so I'm giving it to him with the full
endeavour of
a resolute mortal inclined at times to believe that a totally
different race
has conceived and borne him. I am not from here, not from
here, but
not from there either. For example, which of the following
four possibilities is more convenient, more pleasant or more
correct: For dust thou art and unto
dust shalt thou return. For dust thou art not and unto
dust shalt thou return. For dust thou art and unto
dust thou shalt not
return. For dust thou art not and unto
dust thou shalt not return.
I am misleading Death with the aid of
a complex system of alternatives, yet
because of our intrinsic relationship I only
seem to mislead myself. Any other way out is better than
any other way out, bypassing with a pathetic gesture the
only
way out that I do not wish to know within the present
framework
of my ingresses and egresses, through which I have been
preparing

not to pass since the dawn of my youth, since the dawn of
my self-defending consciousness, commander-in-chief of
the most active private army in my vicinity. Don't go
home this evening, girl. It is, after all, an evening
destined to last forever. It is, in fact, the first
and last evening destined for anything
at all. The inevitable hootings
are already chasing it. Something
transpires in the bowels of the earth, aspires to
something darker than itself though
brighter than itself. Nothing will change, of course, but
I am still, as always, tensed towards the other way out,
    finally prepared
for the takeoff. When the chariot-of-fire
has landed, I wouldn't wish to be found
in a better or worse state than the one I'm in
at this singular hour.

                                              (*Tr.* **A.B.**)

Maxim Ghilan (1931-)

ARS PO

Poetry
Is the infirm's glass, the oldster's staff
The quilt
Across the legs, drawn tight,
The light
Of candles held aloft. The soft
Cry in the night. The knee
Bent against stone, a silent ballad
Below the weight. The sleight
Of hands that must grasp rain
The hidden spatter of furtive, grass-grained
Sheets of pain.

(*Tr.* by the author)

WOMAN IN A RED NIGHTROBE
(Sung on Teleprynter)

THEY WRITE FROM SEATTLE A WOMAN
HAS BEEN FOUND DEAD IN A RED NIGHTROBE
A RED RED ROROBE
A RED NIGHTROBE (MORE)
A WOMAN YOUNG HER HAIR IN ORDER
HER BODY SLEEPING UNDISTURBED
A BULLET HOLE BLUE BURNED ON HER TEMPLE
HER RIGHT YOUNG TEMPLE
QUOTE THE BLOOD WAS RED AROUND HER HEAD
    LIKE
THE RIGHT RED NIGHTROBE UNQUOTE
THE RED RED RED NIGHT QUOTE XXXXX
THUS NEWS FROM SEATTLE THEN STOCK QUO-
    TATIONS
AND THEN HAMMERSHIELD MORE AND MORE
    AND MORE
POLITICAL NEWS ECONOMIC REPORTS AUTO-
    MATIC
RELEASES OF A NIGHT AGAIN PASSED BLANK
ALONE THE GLORIOUS WORK OF RETRANSMIS-
    SION

AND SHE OF THE RED NIGHTROBE
LYING THERE STILL HER HEAD COATED IN RED
    RED
BLOOD LIKE THE RED RED OF THE RED NIGHT-
    ROBE
FLASH NEWS FROM NAGASAKI TELL OF FORTY
    FISHERS
CAUGHT BY THE ATOM STORM THE AFGHAN
    CHIEFLINGS HAVE
PROTESTED AGAIN AGAINST AFGHAN TREACHERY
    IT SEEMS

BUT QUOTE WHERE IS SHE OF THE RED BURN-
 ING NIGHTROBE
INTERROGATION UNQUOTE
QUOTE LYING IN THE MORGUE MORGUE MORGUE
LIE LYING IN THE MORGUE UNQUOTE

JONATHAN OF SPARTA

You have crossed many seas, Jonathan. What God gives to man
You jolly well accept. Well done, at any rate
From time to time, Jonathan.

You ate your fill. Whatever you took in, you did not keep.
The armoury glistened on the ship's dark deck. None but you
 knew

That even steel has its dreams, Jonathan.

They called you a traitor. Well, you were just a creator
Of someone else's pains. The wine was sweet and red.
They yelled you down, they yelled you away.
Now inside your entrails eats the burning dismay

Of the gnawing fox, Jonathan.

(*Tr.* by the author)

TO AN OLD FRIEND

Go to hell.
When you go
I shall bolt the door behind you.
Seven bolts, without a safety-catch, as in the rifle
You carried on your shoulder,
Will bristle from the door, torture-nails in your eyes.
You will go down
Crooked stairs, leading to a long-forgotten tower
And wonder how far you are gone
And remember you have already known
This very day, long ago.

Go to blazes.
My spirits are low like yours,
But your world is better off in its grey shroud
While I am cowed,
Tearing the cover of my world into ragged bands
With my bare hands.

I don't want you in my guts any more.
You are too much my own sore,
Too bloody earnest,
Far too close.
You can take it from me:
Go to hell. Leave me be.

(*Tr.* A.B.)

THIS HEAT WILL

This heat will devour my senses yet.
This heat which has surely met
Nocturnal tasks, my life's remainder.

We go on building all our castles on sand, the threshold of the
wave.
We build within, not understanding and much too weary to
connive.
This heat must know. This heat must grasp it. Must realize what
we have seen.
With it we move as in deep silence. I'll say this clearly: the
khamseen
Invades the kernel of our senses, skyrocketing the price of day
While on the soil of our pretence we walk with fierce untram-
meled joy.
Dip in this heat as in the water. It will engulf us like a wave.
Plunge here. Two hands. A dewy cluster in fists closed tightly
like a cave.
This heat will surely craze my senses, the tongues of my fomented
brain.

This heat. And who can tell for certain its source, or when it goes
   again?
You are the rose of all my summers. Soft petals, open, cool and
   slow.
You, you alone. A cloud of water. I am the wilderness below.
We'll see and touch and taste and swallow, gulp a sweet drink
   from your mouth.
A fountain flowing from a crevice. We drink. Insatiable drouth.
This is your heat. Berserker music. Its tone is shrill and taut and
   mad.
This heat of yours, whom is it greeting? Where does it come
   from, proud and sad?
The grass astir. This tree, our shelter, where we shall hide
   between the aisles.
A sun is blazing. Soon a sheaf of time will crack beneath its flail.
For you I sit in sun-baked mourning. My bloodshot tears upon
   your thighs.
It's you I want, it's you, returning. A fervent dream of summer
   nights.
This heat will craze my weary senses. Myself. Yourself. All that
   is mine.
My hand. Your hand. My day is setting. My life and yours. A
   gutter. Wine.

                                                      (*Tr.* A.B.)

Dan Paggis (1930-   )

THE TOWER

I did not want to tower, but nimble memories
Setting tier upon tier, each to itself,
Stirred in a babel of alien tongues,
Left breaches in me,
Stairs that did not lead to — bitter perspectives.
With no translator to myself, unfinished
I was at last abandoned.
But sometimes, in a crooked corridor
A wordless whisper like a draught
Yet rises in me and yet runs,
And I seem a whirl of dust that for a moment
Rears its head to heaven,
And before I wake
The lump of my burnt bricks crumbles
And returns to dust.

(*Tr.* Miriam Arad)

EPILOGUE TO ROBINSON CRUSOE

From an island heavy with parrots and forgotten by speech
He's back, as if he'd paused for a day
Till the lucky wind came. He's back and here he is.
But at the door
The years turned suddenly on hinges. And then,
Between empty chairs, he knew
What had happened in the meantime, and grew wise
Like someone who has no return.
Too wise to live, gray-haired and dry he lived
With the clay-pipe of his stories, and he spoke —
To dull the ticking of his dead
And their chiming — he spoke and spoke
Of an island unchanged and still waiting for shipwrecks.

(*Tr.* Dennis Silk)

THE EXPERIMENT

At an hour of perspicuity he traced
as in an alchemist's pellucid phial
the transmutations of his body. In his veins
A fiery quicksilver throbbed. He forced
his glance to penetrate the hiding-place
where, like a spider in its web, surprised,
his heart hung in the balance,
a lethal particle. A wicked light
toyed with a grain of gold, a taper
that flickered for a while and fizzled out.
But when outdoors, impatient, quick to bloom,
something sprang up
and flayed the window like an April storm,
he saw at last: one should begin like that.
This trial he could stand. The mysteries
whose combination faltered he

summarily dismissed. That he should grow
in peace, he now unravelled all his knots
and shrank into a modicum of dust.

(*Tr.* A.B.)

AGAIN A WITNESS

Again a witness, I am bound and I pass
Through pale electric day, scurry through rain
Between quarrels of wires — another street
Always for the time being —
And inside to a film gray with love, its heroes
Long dead before the hall
of empty chairs, hall of shadows.

Again a witness, and I leave the last tube.
The night quiet, in some back-quarter
Of the double-dealing town, its branches
Pushing their shadows into
The mist. An alley I went round,
A wrought iron gate I didn't open.

Had I stayed, who would have saved me
From my heart's fist? A stranger
With a turned-up collar in November's wind,
Caught in the thicket of my veins, with someone else
And later than I, keeping in step with me
At every instant before hate.
My sentence. I am bound and I pass.

(*Tr.* Dennis Silk)

IN THE DEAD VILLAGE

Coming to the cindered stillness,
To the stones and plaster of walls,
To the village lying dead and headless

Where the trembling ash still falls,
And among the thistles murmurs still linger
While overhead memory's clouds
Wake and rise, heavy with anger, —
Suddenly hate's falcon dives,
Spreading wings like a cross to view,
And its talons, blades of sun,
Your footsteps pursue.

(*Tr.* Dov Vardi)

BATTLE

With eyes big and strange
And fractured brow,
The dead beside their pits will range,
Slowly assembling row on row
Beyond the ledge of fear.
Speechless they'll stand with gaping jaw:
It cannot be known who is blessed, who accursed
In the scorched earth.

(*Tr.* Dov Vardi)

ARARAT

When all the Ark's survivors burst ashore
And in a frenzy of delight
Jumped, chattered, roared for prey
And bellowed procreation,
The rainbow beaconing above their heads
That no more ends would come — it was the end
For those prehensile, carefree fish, they who had thriven
Upon the tragedy, quick-witted profiteers
Who now were trapped in a congealing earth
And, lashing tail and fin,
With mouths agape, were drowning in the air.

(*Tr.* A.B.)

Dalia Ravikovitz (1936-)

THE BLUE LIZARD IN THE SUN

A lizard lay in the sun and it had a blue tail-end.
The patch of grasses beside it looked big as a forest land,
But the sun, the good sun, seemed as small as a grain of
 sand.

The marvellous sun that caresses tail and front,
That slakes our thirst like a cool, delicious pond,
A sun like the golden playball of which the young are so
 fond.

Her love reaches for their bodies with fingers light and fair,
Her warmth like bunches of bubbles soars up in the air,
And when she shines from above, the lizards' backs flare

And become a medley of colours: blue and red and golden,
And watching her glow from the treetops the lizards behold
 then
How the leaves grow yellow and how the resin grows
 molten.

Then will the big trees with shame and atonement retreat.
The grass will prostrate itself humbly at Mother Earth's feet,
And none but the lizards will relish the sun's glorious heat.

A lizard lay on a stone and it had a blue tail-end.
The patch of grasses beside it looked big as a forest land,
But the sun, the good sun, seemed to shrink like a grain
    of sand.

                                              (*Tr.* A.B.)

WICKED PALM

Lines of smoke stretched out aslant
And my daddy gave me a beating.
Those who stood by laughed at the sight.
What I am telling is perfectly true.

Lines of smoke stretched out aslant
And my daddy struck me on the palm of my hand.
It was a wicked palm, he said.
What I am telling is perfectly true.

Lines of smoke stretched out aslant.
My daddy no longer beat me.
The wicked palm grew five long fingers.
Whatever it did was established and firm.

Lines of smoke stretched out aslant.
Fear is grazing the wicked palm.
My daddy no longer gives me a beating
But this fear of mine is established and firm.

                                              (*Tr.* A.B.)

SHUNRA*

Shunra was white and pink like a frosted cake.
She had been to London. she had been to Moscow.
All her days were one long Sabbath with plenty

* *Shunra* — Aramaic for cat.

Of clouds, but her garden flourished from day to day.
When it rained the house leaked through a roof of glass;
She went up to the window. Somebody was waiting for her.
He was reading a letter but she addled his wits,
So he put it aside and kissed her like a frosted cake.
It was rather late in the morning
And he smacked his lips all day long, all day long.
Shunra spread a napkin on her knees and sat down to lap
    up a vanilla cake.

(Tr. A.B.*)*

THE VAGARIES OF TIME

For fifteen years he had been clinging to his pages
Until a crown of dampness sprouted on his head.
Between two pavements a fat thorn grew up
And cats gave birth to kittens every year
(The little ones were quick to climb the parapets).

The rivers of the sea were simmering at dusk.
By morning all Creation was at breaking-point.
He knew the vagaries of the four seasons
(The ravages of winter healed by spring).

For fifteen years he had been clinging to his pages
And fledgelings twittered from their nest into his ear.
He also had a rumour of some earthquake
And he would cry for those unfortunates
Who perished, nor forgot the roar of waters.
At times he noticed, to his great delight,
A moon as round and king-size as a tub.
But once he halted in his tracks and saw
A great wind wafting seeds, innumerable seeds.

(Tr. A.B.*)*

Moshé Dor (1932-   )

VERDICT

The shores of your dream are beyond the reach of the flesh.
The bulrushes stoop over the black, heavy brink
Of the water. I cry out in terror, engulfed, enmeshed—
Not a ripple appears in the place where I sink.

The hand clutches madly at reeds, at darkness and water:
No succour,
No answer,
Not a breath of air on the sore-bitten lips.
Distant ram's horns soar up to the Mount of Slaughter,
And the prayer-shawls of the Jews are spread all over the pits.

The chin grows numb. The warm eyeblood in the final chill
    trembles.
Awake, Jezebel, Cleopatra, any of that God-damned batch!
The ram's horn tears at the eardrums, crushes against the
    temples,
And the yellowish eyes of the Jews are inflamed, match by match.

293

Is this why I have to die, to be called to account?
I just wanted to witness Jezebel's dream, Elijah's chariot of fire —
My nose has no hook, yet they'll wrap me up in a shroud
Having hauled me against the stone-blind moon in my pearly
    attire.

You will never awake.
Sombre and hushed I am crossing the bounds of the carnal
    domain.
The ram's horns are still, the prayer-shawls rustle no more in the
    dark.
The mouth cannot mumble its song. The watermark fades from
    the brain.
Only my yellowish eyes flicker aimlessly like insensate sparks.

(*Tr.* A.B.)

BLACK ROSE

The darkness that will soon discharge aquatic secrets
Is a black rose.
The lightnings sprouting from its heart refute
All floral-faunal theories.
Now, having grown accustomed to the horse's whinny
He feels, bare-headed, gravel-blind,
The thunder's gallop on realities no longer valid.
Ignoring every sacrosanct convention
He manages to fuse the bristled glass,
To penetrate the heart of the black rose.
Freed of self-pity,
Endowed with heavens clean of complexes,
Of raging sex delirium,
Of cancer gnawing at a time-old trunk,
He hides the lightnings in the deep blood's caverns
Where they shall flourish in due course
Like those black roses
On golden pillars.

(*Tr.* A.B.)

UNICORNS

Unicorns ran back and forth upon my eyelids,
Skipping wide rivers of research.
Zoology's breath was short, her face livid,
her arteries swollen with rage.
I caressed their bristling necks,
Their eyes were all over mine.
O my mythlings,
I shall never never trade you
For all the bicorns in the world.

(*Tr.* A.B.)

Ory Bernstein (1936-   )

PENELOPE

The colour of her hair was like the tint
of old wood. She forgot her hands like gloves
upon a folded dress. Swift-winged like doves
her thoughts would hurtle through his wanderings,
creating by their noise the gift of silence.
And while she waited all those chilly nights
her life was singled out by alien hands,
her life still walked and walked around those hours
when he had wandered in her body's lands.
But time flows on. Time never stands aloof.
The armchair was becoming her domain.
She would not budge. Her very breath came sparse.
Her thoughts were counted one by one like beads
in a decrepit, rotund rosary.
Now she was bounded, reconciled. Only her eyes
still followed him like a knife in his back
through his conceited voyages that stretched
to continents no longer strange to her.

(*Tr.* A.B.)

BIRDS HAVE THOUGHTS

Birds have thoughts
when passing from wind to wind.
How they would like to rescind
their motion! But fraught
with their own self-importance
and their soaring prestige
in the nubilous sphere,
they fly. At the tip of their wing, though,
tiredness flits like a portent.
Birds have thoughts
expressed in flight
not in speech.
And when they give up the sky
and lie
among the stones
and chill sprouts in their bones,
a sharp thought pecks at each
tiny brain: if they can make up a system
maybe those wings won't be so heavy
when the winds twist them.
Celestial stability
demands ever-young wings —
a thought beyond the scope
of birdlike ability,
a thought with which they can't cope.
So the birds are assailed
by the light where everything might happen,
so their bodies grow cold and misshapen,
and all their thoughts are of no avail
against death.

(*Tr.* A.B.)

A PORTRAIT

There is a son, too. An inveterate
chain-smoker, emaciated by responsibilities. At night
he still roams alone in the realms of amber,
clears a forest or two, crosses an ocean, can still remember
how, marching with the crowd, he held onto friends.
Now all these dreams are past. He still wants a home,
but a higher judge, sitting on some unearthly throne,
has decreed to put him in chains. Now he has no use
for friendships easy to win and easy to lose.
He withdraws into himself. Even the females
are imposed on him like terms of penal
servitude, to be served one by one.
He has a private fate. He throws his portion
of memories overboard, like an anchor, but the ocean
spews up its spume and washes them ashore.
He is a perennial son, will never be a father.
He is a cul-de-sac, a state of relaxation,
sealing one by one those days of the before.

(Tr. A.B.*)*

AFTER THE BLOWS

After the blows, when I was struck down like grass
By dint of the walking eye,
The supple hips, the streamlined form,
Somebody warned
Not to forgive. Somebody traced
Magic circles round Revenge
That it shall not differ, that it shall not die,
That it shall conform.

To hate is *not* to relent,
Not to change like a wave round a rock

Nor live like a clinging ivy, but
That the body should revive and mock,
That resolutions should melt and the blood
Should sprout again after harvest,
And silently, from a far-off gate,
The tide should come flooding in.

Whoever forbade goes on to hurl
A winglike shadow over the hills
And lift it big. Slothful.

Embarrassed.

And the clouds get dizzy and begin to swirl.

(*Tr.* A.B.)

Arnon Ben-Nahum (1930-   )

RETURN

A moon rises like a bubble
Over the mountains of Edom:
An ancient bronze-jar, refulgent,
Engraved in Arabian script.

And I,
A conscientious rock-explorer,
Have come to gauge the boundary-line,
The plateau's treadmill,
The lowland's extremities,
In a buttoned landscape
On a mystified night.

The moon is going up
And I am coming down to you.
I rejoin you
Yet have no rejoinder.

I am your kin,
A blighted reed, mossless,
Unwilling to see a road paved,
A bud bloom,
A false dream wither.

You are bound.
Your blood sizzles,
Your blood blazes.
You are a flame of thirst,
You are a pristine urge,
A savage glossary,
A bright eye-pupil, voracious,
Unrelenting.

A moon ascending
Over Edom
And I am coming
Down again

To fall into your lap,
Be blighted by your light,
The reed-slayer.

                              (*Tr.* A.B.)

EAGLE

The old,
Long-winged,
Large-plumed eagle
Has lost his spectacles,
The ancient eagle.

A burning pain
Imprinted on his eyes,
On the sinew of his cheek.
His plume is bristling.

In his talon is whetted
A primal wrath,
A blind, destructive
Surgent wrath.

Search every lintel,
Every doorpost:
His life is at stake.

(*Tr.* A.B.)

Meir Wieseltier (1941-)

LEMMUS LEMMUS

I live in Scandinavia. I am
lemmus lemmus, length 13 cm. tail
1 or 2 cm. I am plain as a mouse.
I dwell in the mountains and nibble grass
and my spouse litters 5 brats
twice a year.

One day I wake up with the sea in my bones
but I dare not go there alone.
My dad and granddad on the same weathered track
went north to the sea and never came back.

Lemmus lemmus, go to sea.
Lemmus lemmus, go to sea.
On your way they'll hound you
And the water will drown you.

I draw closer and closer to my spouse.
She says she understands me, at least

she loves me with all her heart.
And she begins to litter every month:
brats, brats, brats like sand
on the seashore, ten a litter.
My spouse never dies in childbirth.

Now I know: there is no resort.
Lemmus lemmus' semen is thus absorbed
only once in a great many years. Very soon
the sea will spew up my household's boon.

Farewell, Scandinavia, we sail away!
We are lemmus lemmus, lovers of seas,
breakers, sunset on mighty waters.

(Tr. A.B.)

SHOWER AFTER FIRST DEATH

Cold Shower after first death,
I am waiting for you. Beyond my friends' grieved palms,
Beyond my forthcoming poem, somewhere you
Hold back your flow towards our great day,
Damp your sounds until our festive day.
Cold shower after first death,
I am keeping for you hours of air and fire, while you
Hold the water for me. Think of my curly hair,
My bathos from ecstasy. In the roads of your domain
I am already on the move, will soon break into a trot,
Proliferate my energies on thousands of solar years.

(Tr. A.B.)

BALLAD

I killed a fly with the Poems of Cummings.
It was morning, early in the morning
And my loins were still throbbing off you
(But my heart and eyes were aching)

And the book in my hands was rather loose,
And I crushed a fly with the Poems of Cummings.

The fly preferred the flesh to the inanimate,
The ceiling was left blank without its dominant black spot.
My nose for a while, then straight into the pages,
Like someone unaware of Minos' architectomania;
And this happened quite early in the morning,
And I crushed a fly with the Poems of Cummings.

When I open the book after a long nap,
Followed by a good afternoon breakfast,
The fly will drop, no longer pertinent.
Yet it's somewhat hard, I suppose, to account
For a fly I killed with the Poems of Cummings.

                                        (*Tr.* A.B.)

EXUVIATION

I am thinking how I shall have to slough off my skin
Again, like the good snake spewing its inevitable venom,
But in the fine, well-sniffed spring
It sloughs off its skin with slow, undulate motions
Like a ship.

I am rather impatient to see that lovely day,
To know the new grass on my body and cheeks, to breathe
        air,
Air. I hear innumerable frogs enliven the ponds
And something in me has gone off on a long, rejuvenated,
Unshrinking journey.

I am ready for this day, I am waiting. And when it comes
Then I can say I'm dreaming, and bashfulness will retreat
From the onslaught of returning storks.

                                        (*Tr.* A.B.)

GRAPHOLOGISTS

Those graphologists threaten me:
They examine my hands'· idiosyncrasies
Under the trained eye
Of a magnifying glass, then say:
This sort of thing will come to no good end
And there's a quirk of hatred towards the world
And something very wrong that started long ago.

The pen is poised in my hand, the bench is lit
And long ago something here had a start
And if you call it end you won't be dubbed a liar.
There is a host of dormice stalking man:
With patience and consistency not of this world,
Not from our street, with no specifications
For our postmen. There is a host of dormice
That never fall asleep, never forget.
(Somnolent graphologists don't distinguish its hubbub
From streetcleaners with broomsticks, swishing, slow.
And they see nothing but a distorted end
And it's no good.

But any dormouse can distinguish very well.
Dormice do distinguish this, no doubt).

I must believe, a man said to himself.
A man said, I must believe. So he said.

(*Tr.* A.B.)

Dalia Hertz (1942-   )

MARGOT

I, too, for the last few hours at least, wanted to be like Margot.
We agreed to meet at the café. I was late. Margot was even
  later —
By fully ten minutes. The gist of the matter is I'd like to be
Almost exactly like you, Margot. It isn't easy. I was referred to
  you
And told that you could help me. But you can hardly be
  expected
To show interest. Never mind, I can wait. The water flows
Under the floor. A cheesy summer claws its disgraces.
O yes, I'll try. Margot asks me to excuse her. She must go
To the john for a moment. The other night she hung up on a line
All her scales, the snowy skein. Now she's reluctant to lend
  them.
What does it depend on? I ask her. Margot comes back. I try to
  help.
She coughs. I'll repeat my words. I'd like to be almost exactly

Like you, Margot. Such a well-balanced will, excellent, impec-
cable.
What can I do about it? People remember me as I've always
been.
I buried an axe under my house. Mama is flippant, Papa is
ageing fast.
Margot asks my forgiveness. My heart cries out for her.
She's got to telephone her owner. I can wait, dear Margot.

(*Tr.* A.B.)

THE WHIP-WALKER

They're expecting a chap who walks on a whip. At first
    glance
One might think the chap walks on a rope. This is absurd.
He walks on a whip. But I don't believe it. Nobody does.

The rumour is slow to spread. There's no punch to it.
If a person walks on a whip while everyone else walks on
    a rope
He must have his reasons. If he declines to walk on a rope
There must be a reason. There simply has to be.

By now the public has taken fright. The very thought is
    appalling.

(*Tr.* A.B.)

MACCARENA

I stroll in the gardens where Maccarena withered.
In falsehood, said her cicisbeos, in falsehood the roof's pigeons
Were striving to thrive while you, Maccarena, had leisure to
    wither.

Her father, too, sits on the quilts worn thin by Maccarena.
Her father asks no questions. He knows under whose legs

Maccarena has spread her quilts. He knows about it all.
The same base pity in which your cicisbeos enlaced you,
The same base pity returns to face you.

Hurray, Maccarena, your father hears nothing.
Your father hears nothing, said her cicisbeos.
You shall go with me, Father, to count your descendants.
With my own eyes I saw the nakedness of fathers
And was sick of it and so was Maccarena.

You were our foundling in the cellared roofs,
Your putrid flesh had no sinew, no cinder,
Only naked fathers flitted before your eyes.
Your pigeons are striving to thrive in their gardens.
How grandly, Maccarena, you soared up while I roared
With pleasure, for good measure denied the train of my robe.

Even my putrid flesh, said Maccarena,
Even my putrid flesh will not betray me.

Here's to life, said her cicisbeos,
Her whole life is yet before her,
And I strolled in the gardens where Maccarena withered.

(*Tr.* A.B.)

SEIZURE

I've got a seizure.
I suffer from epilepsy and amnesia.
They come and go together. Under my jaw
There's a thick neck. My face expands by a thermal law.
Now, for instance, I have a seizure. My blood snaps to
    attention.
If someone were to talk to me about oblivion and hyper-
    tension
I should suffer terribly. I might even fall back.
Under my head there bulges a thickening neck.

This weakens my stronghold. I wanted it to grow longer.
I think I have already said I've got a seizure.
I think I'm sinking. I'm enclosed. I attack.

(*Tr.* A.B.)

Glossary and General Notes

A. = Arabic
Ar. = Aramaic
G. = German
E. = English
H. = Hebrew
L. = Latin
R. = Russian
Y. = Yiddish

Aggadáh — The general term given to the legends, folklore, proverbs, adages etc. in the Talmud and the Midrashim (sing. Midrash). For a detailed discussion of the Aggadah see Part III of the Introduction.

Aramaic — A term applied to any one of the northern branch of the semitic family of languages. More particularly, to the dialect spoken by the Jews who returned from the Babylonian exile and settled in Palestine.

Large tracts of the Talmud and other religious literature were written in Aramaic. In recent times this language has served as a remarkable reservoir from which modern Hebrew derived new roots and forms and assimilated them with comparative ease.

Bel — One of the chief gods in ancient Babylon.

Bezbozhnik (R).—A spitefully godless person.

Diaspora (E. fr. Greek) — Dispersion, esp. that of the Jews in the lands of their exile.

Dvekút (H). — Heartfelt piousness bordering on ecstasy. This was one of the salient qualities of the Hassidic movement.

Gemarah (H.) — The Talmudic amplification of the legal points initiated by the Mishna. The Gemarah is mainly written in Aramaic.

Gentile (E.) — A non-Jewish person. In modern usage this term is purely technical.

Halakhah (H.) — The legal, technical and instructive part of the Talmud and other books of religious literature. Note that Halakhah and Aggadah are not contradictory but complementary, sometimes overlapping.

Haskaláh (H.) — A Hebrew word meaning 'education' and also 'enlightment.' The Haskalah Movement sought to acquaint the Jews of Eastern Europe with secular subjects and professions.

Hassidic Movement — A semi-mysterious, religious movement which arose among the Jews of Eastern Europe in the eighteenth century. The Hebrew word 'Hassid' means a pious person. The Hassidic Movement was founded by Rabbi Israel *Baal-Shem-Tov* (known by his initials as *'The Besht'*).

"He became the leader of a cult. . . .called Hassidism, and its central tenet was the belief that everything — mind and matter, good and evil, the birds and trees and rocks and rills — everything was a manifestation of God. From this it followed that God could be worshipped anywhere, and not necessarily according to a fixed formula, but with whatever words came into one's mind. The most ignorant man, therefore, could draw as near to God as the most learned. And since access to God was so easy, one ought to be full of joy; one ought to sing and dance and get mildly drunk on occasion. *Hassidism* was a sort of mass evangelical movement, intensely fervid, revivalistic, antinomian, anticlerical, democratic, superstitious — and comforting."

(from *The Wisdom of Israel*, ed. Lewis Browne, p.452, The New English Library Ltd., by courtesy of the publishers)

Kamerad (G.) — Comrade, especially a comrade-at-arms.

Ka-Tzetnik — An inmate of a concentration or extermination camp. The author of *The Clock Overhead* was one of those inmates at Auschwitz.

Khamsin (A.) — A hot eastern desert wind prevalent in Israel and the neighbouring countries during certain seasons of the year.

Kohen (or Cohen, pl. Kohanim or Cohanim) — A Hebrew word meaning 'a priest.' Ever since the Second Temple was destroyed a *cohen* means a man who is descended from those priests. The Rabbinical law imposes on a *cohen* stricter limitations than on the layman insofar as marriage is concerned. He cannot, for instance, marry a divorcée, hence the delicate point raised by the *cohanim* in Bialik's 'The City of Slaughter.'

Ladino — A Spanish dialect, interspersed with Hebrew words and idioms, spoken by Sephardic Jews in the Middle East (including Israel), the Balkan countries, North Africa and elsewhere.

Levite (H.) — Originally, one of the tribe of Levi. The Levites had no tribal estate of their own in ancient Israel but were dedicated to the works of the Temple. Their duties included singing sacred hymns and playing various instruments. After the fall of the Second Temple the term was applied to their descendants.

Matan Toráh (H.) — The Revelation of Mount Sinai, where the Toráh (the Sacred Law) was given to the people of Israel. (Lit. The Giving of the Toráh).

Massadáh (H.) — The name of the famous bastion near the Dead Sea that held against the Romans long after the Second Temple had fallen. In Isaac Lamdan's long poem of the same name, Massadah is used symbolically to denote the dauntless spirit of the Pioneers who settled in Palestine. The word 'Massad' means a foundation. In recent years the real Massadah has become world-renowned because of the important archaeological excavations carried out by scientists and laymen alike.

Meggido (H.) — An ancient town in Israel where King Solomon's stables were situated. It is in the Valley of Meggido, at the foot of *Har-Meggido* (The Mount of Meggido, known as *Armaggedon*) that the final battle is to take place, according to Christian belief, before the Day of Judgement.

Midrash (H., pl. *Midrashim*) — A collection of Aggadah stories, homilies etc. which were not included in the Talmud but were regarded as a kind of non-legal sequel to it.

Pilpul (H.) — Ludicrous hairsplitting and casuistry.

Pogrom (R.) — A murderous riot against the Jews, esp. one instigated by the 'Black Hundreds,' the police of the Czarist regime at the end of the nineteenth century.

Rosh-Ha-Shana (H.) — The Jewish New Year.

Sabra (A., H. *Tsabar*) A nickname for an Israeli-born person, based on the name of the cactus-fruit which is thorny on the outside but soft and sweet inside.

Shabbat (H., Y. *Shabbes*), Saturday, the Jewish Sabbath.

Sharav (H.) — Sultry weather, incl. *khamsin*.

Shekel (H.) — An ancient Hebrew coin of silver or gold.

Shohet (H.) — A Jewish ritual slaughterer.

Shtreiml (Y. fr. Polish) — A broad, round felt hat worn till recently by the Jews of Eastern Europe.

Swipple (E.) — The part of the flail that strikes the grain in thrashing.

Tabernacle (E. fr. L.) — A small hut covered with shrubbery, erected each year in the Jewish house for the eight days which constitute the Feast of *Sukkoth* (Tabernacles).

Talmud (H.) — The body of Jewish civil and ceremonial traditionary law, containing both Halakhah and Aggadah.

Wellaway (E., also 'welladay') — An archaic exclamation expressing sorrow or lamentation, like 'alas.'

Wiedergutmachung (G.) — Lit. 'setting things right' — reparations, esp. those extended to world Jewry and to the Government of Israel by the Government of the German Federal Republic as compensation for the loss of life and property caused to millions of Jews by the Nazi persecutions.

Yiddish — The language spoken by Jews in Eastern Europe and brought from there to various parts of the world. Yiddish comprises mainly German and Hebrew elements.

Yishuv — The Jewish community in Palestine, before and during the British Mandate.

Yom Kippur (H.) — The Jewish Day of Atonement on which they fast and pray in order to atone for the year's sins.

Zohar (H. for 'splendour') — Title of a cabalistic work introduced in the thirteenth century by Rabbi Moshé de Leon and ascribed to the ancient sage Rabbi Shimon Bar-Yokhai.

Bibliography

Note: This Bibliography includes mainly those works available in English which contain or deal with Hebrew poetry from Bialik on.

AUSUBEL, Nathan, *A Treasury of Jewish Folklore,* Crown 1948.
AUSUBEL, Nathan and Marynn, *A Treasury of Jewish Poetry,* Crown, New York, 1957.
BIALIK, Hayyim, *Complete Works,* ed. Israel Efros, Histadruth Ivrith of America, New York, 1948.
————, *Poems from the Hebrew,* ed. L. V. Snowman, London, 1924.
————, *Selected Poems,* ed. Maurice Samuel, New York, 1926.
BROWNE, Lewis, *The Wisdom of Israel,* New English Library, London, 1962.
FEIN, Harry, *A Harvest of Hebrew Verse,* Bruce Humphries Inc., Boston, 1934.
FLEG, Edmond, *The Jewish Anthology,* tr. Maurice Samuel. Behrman's Jewish Book House, New York, 1940.
HAEZRAHI, Yehudah ed., Modern Hebrew Poetry (duplicated edition), The Federation of Zionist Youth, London.
HALKIN, S. *Modern Trends in Hebrew Literature.* Schocken Books, New York, 1950.

ISRAEL ARGOSY, Nos. 1-7, ed. I. Halevy-Levin, Jerusalem, Israel.

RIBALOW, Menachem, *The Flowering of Modern Hebrew Literature,* ed. & tr. Judah Nadich, Vision Pres, London, 1959.

SCHWARZ Leo W., *A Golden Treasury of Jewish Literature,* Farrar & Rinehart, New York, 1937.

SHALOM, Shin, *On Ben Peleh,* Youth and Hehalutz Department of the Zionist Organization, Jerusalem, 1963.

SHIMONI, David, *Idylls,* tr. I. M. Lask, ibid., Jerusalem, 1957.

SIFRUT, Nos. 1-3, ed. C. Rabin and D. Patterson, Jewish Agency Dept. for Education and Culture, London, 1956.

SNOWMAN, L.V., ed. & tr., *Tchernichovsky and his Poetry,* London, 1929.

VARDI, Dov, *New Hebrew Poetry,* WIZO Instruction Centre, Tel Aviv, 1947.

WALLENROD, Reuben, *The Literature of Modern Israel,* Abelard-Schuman, New York, 1957.

Index to Poets and Titles

318

Library
Brevard Junior College
Cocoa, Florida